lettering by
JOHN DRANSKI

introduction by
JAMIE S. RICH

book design by
KEITH WOOD

collection edited by
JAMES LUCAS JONES

original series edited by
JAMIE S. RICH &
JAMES LUCAS JONES

Published by Oni Press, Inc.

JOE NOZEMACK, publisher

JAMES LUCAS JONES, senior editor

RANDAL C. JARRELL, managing editor

IAN SHAUGHNESSY, editorial intern

Mike Hawthorne would like to thank Despina Hawthorne and Erik Swanson for all the help and support; Adrian Brown, Antony Johnston, and Kieron Gillen for the reference help; and Alex Toth, Alex Raymond, Jordi Bernet and Nina Simone for getting him through the long nights drawing.

Original Queen & Country logo designed by
STEVEN BIRCH @ Servo

This collects issues 21-24 of the Oni Press comics series *Queen & Country*™.

ONI PRESS, INC.
6336 SE Milwaukie Avenue, PMB30
Portland, OR 97202
USA

www.onipress.com • www.gregrucka.com

First edition: August 2004
ISBN 1-929998-97-X

1 3 5 7 9 10 8 6 4 2

PRINTED IN CANADA.

INTRODUCTION

by JAMIE S. RICH

It's time to be honest with ourselves.

Just like most of us barely use 10% of our brains, most of us barely know 10% of what goes on in the world. Those numbers aren't scientific, and the second one in particular is entirely made up by me; I'd wager it's being generous, too. In fact, I should probably clarify it to be that we know 10% of what is reported about what goes on in the world, because there is a hell of a lot more that happens that is not mentioned in places that the general public can hear it.

There's not much excuse for this. With the variety of ways information travels around the planet these days, it's easier than ever to find out what is going on. Granted, you have to sift through a lot of debris to get to the treasure, but to not do so is just willful ignorance. We'd rather live in denial and blame a crappy mainstream media and carry on with what we consider to be a normal life free from the fears and frustrations that may be going on thousands of miles from our homes.

It's a thin veneer, though. Consider as you read this volume of *Queen & Country* how easily you believe Greg Rucka's work of fiction. As events unfold and you learn the many ways one government is manipulating another, and how factions of the same government are even working towards opposite results of one another, consider how effortlessly you swallow this pill. Forces inside a major world power are stage-managing the course of politics in a country smaller than they are, and it seems perfectly normal to our modern eyes.

And yet, we go to bed each night thinking that, really, the powers that be are working in our best interest, they aren't out to harm us.

We know bad things go on behind closed doors, but we choose to let them go on. It shouldn't allow us to feel as safe and comfortable as we do, but we carry on with the attitude that everything will be fine. "God's in His heaven, and all is right in the world...even if we can't agree on the specifics of this God or His kingdom"

I suppose part of this is necessary. How many of us would lose our ability to function if we openly admitted to ourselves that these kinds of things go on everyday with very little there to stop it, much less monitor it? No one wants to accept that they are a single piece of plankton in a vast ocean of fish of increasingly larger sizes and predatory natures. It's not a very correct or good way to approach life, but it's not impossible to understand.

Queen & Country is about the people that fully face the realities the common citizenry cannot. It's about the hands of the unseen hands, who reach out across the world to do what they feel must be done. It's a moody and grey world about often mean and restless people who don't always act in accordance with what they think is right. Sometimes it's about doing what you think you must do at the time, about giving the devil you know a leg up rather than face the alternative.

Of course, to make this comic book work, it requires that Greg Rucka fully face the reality that his characters can't avoid. It requires him to look beyond the 10% that the rest of us are content to know, to seek out the other 90% and move beyond it, try to fathom the unknowable. He probably sleeps less comfortably, but he does it for the same reason his characters do—because he knows something must be done. Someone has to be paying attention. For him to give it any less would be to let not just his readership down, but these fictional constructs, these avatars of human beings, that he has brought to life.

To complete his mission, he enlists only the best. Mike Hawthorne is the latest in a long line of soldiers to work in Greg's Special Section. Whether or not he is the greatest is up to personal taste, but I can say he is probably the most thorough. Just about every moment in this story has been researched to death. When Tara and Tom go to Bath, those are real shops you are seeing. Mike got people to go and take pictures. He even worried about getting the right kind of songbird in the background. That's dedication!

So, make no mistake, Greg and Mike have done the work for you. They have sought out the things that you know you need to know and made the inquiries you're afraid to make; they've made the gathering of this knowledge easier on you. To enter these pages, though, is to enter a pact. Your thanks extend beyond the price you paid for this book. For what you get between these covers, you owe it to them to stop looking at the world the same way, to start asking more questions and remove some of the burden from Greg, his collaborators, and their characters. None of us are in this alone, so don't be the one to drop the ball.

You've got 90% more brainspace than you're putting to use. You've got the room. No excuses.

Jamie S. Rich
notes from the overground
July 5, 2004

The former editor in chief of Oni Press and original editor of Queen & Country, *Jamie S. Rich is now a member of the private sector, working away on his second prose novel,* The Everlasting. *Hopefully it's not news to you that he has a first novel, but if it is, for your information it's called* Cut My Hair *and the fine folks at Oni still have a couple of copies. He can be visited on the web at www.confessions123.com.*

CHAPTER 1

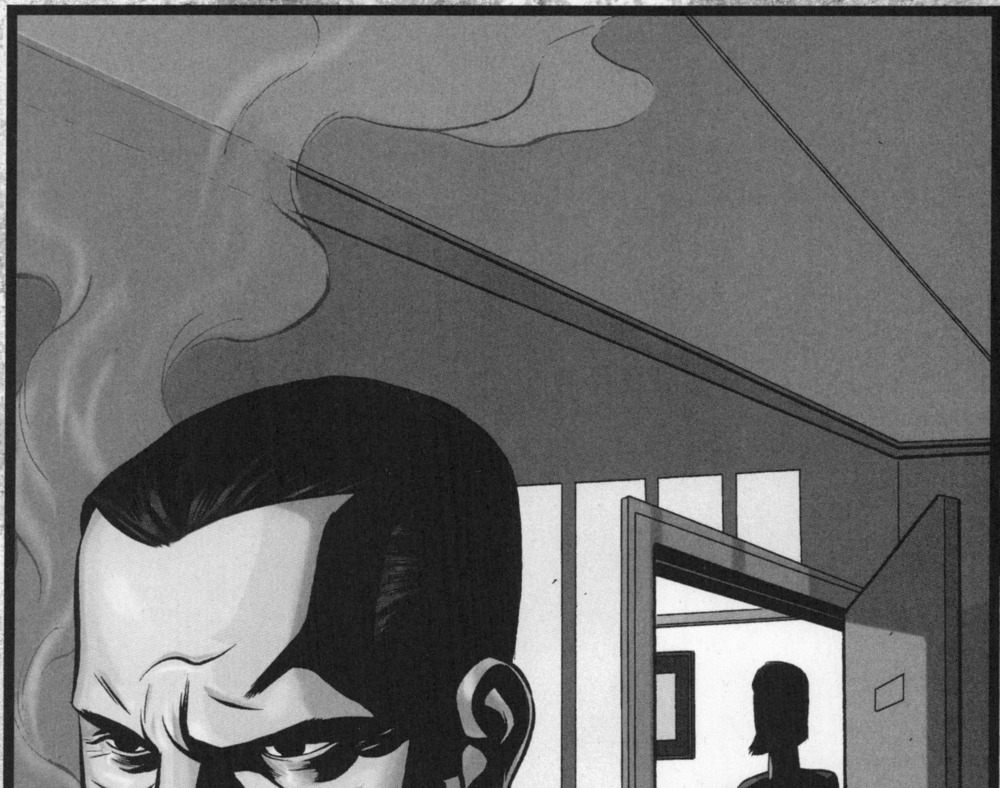

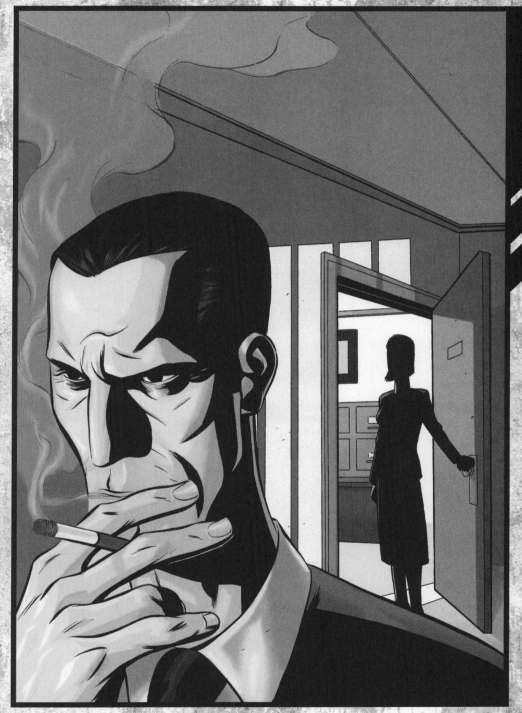

ROSTER

TARA CHACE

Special Operations Officer, designated Minder Two. Entering her third year as Minder.

FRANCES BARCLAY

Chief of Service, also known as 'C.' Distinguished service as CIA-Liaison, Chairman of the Joint Intelligence Committee, and as Head of Station Prague (85-88), Saigon (89-91), and Paris (91-94).

TOM WALLACE

Head of the Special Section, a Special Operations Officer with the designation Minder One. Responsible for the training and continued well-being of his unit, both at home and in the field. Six year veteran of the Minders.

PAUL CROCKER

Director of Operations, encompassing all field work in all theaters of operations.

In addition to commanding individual stations, has direct command of the Special Section—sometimes referred to as Minders—used for special operations.

C

Ubiquitous code-name for the current head of S.I.S. Real name is Sir Wilson Stanton Davies.

DONALD WELDON

Deputy Chief of Service, has oversight of all aspects of Intelligence gathering and operations. Immediate superior to Crocker.

OPS ROOM STAFF:

KATE

Personal Assistant to Paul Crocker, termed P.A. to D.Ops. Possibly the hardest and most important job in the Service.

RON

Duty Operations Officer, responsible for monitoring the status and importance of all incoming intelligence, both from foreign stations and other sources.

ALEXIS

Mission Control Officer (also called Main Communications Officer)—responsible for maintaining communications between the Operations Room and the agents in the field.

OTHERS:

WALTER SECCOMBE

Permanent Under Secretary to the Foreign Office, a career civil servant with intimate knowledge of the inner workings of all levels of Government, and with the savvy to negotiate the corridors of power to achieve his own ends.

EDWARD KITTERING

Special Operations Officer, designated Minder Three. Has been with the Special Section for less than a year.

DECEASED

BRIAN BUTLER

A former sergeant in one of the British Army's oldest and most respected regiments. An unique individual who actually requested assignment with special section.

DECEASED

LONDON.

COGNAC AND CIGARS?

IT'S THE LOUIS XIII, DECANTED FROM THE BACCARAT.

DELIGHTFUL, THANK YOU.

TWO OF THE *COHIBAS* FROM MY *HUMIDOR*, PLEASE, REG.

VERY GOOD, SIR.

I THOUGHT THE WELLINGTON WAS PASSABLE. PERHAPS A TAD *RARE*.

HMM? VERY GOOD, YES, WALTER.

YOU NEVER TOLD ME, FRANCES. HOW WAS *WASHINGTON*?

OH, I THOUGHT QUITE PRODUCTIVE, QUITE USEFUL. DIANE ENJOYED IT, CERTAINLY.

YOU KNOW HOW IT IS WITH THE AMERICANS, THAT FEROCIOUS NEED TO LEAP FIRST AND ASK QUESTIONS *LATER*.

I DO, I DO *INDEED*.

STILL, AN *IMPORTANT* RELATIONSHIP, WITHOUT A DOUBT. PERHAPS *THE* IMPORTANT RELATIONSHIP, ESPECIALLY NOW, NO?

AH, YES.

QUITE.

YOU *HEARD* ABOUT SIR WILSON, OF COURSE.

YES. IT'S... UNFORTUNATE. HE WAS AN EXCEPTIONAL *C*.

I UNDERSTAND HE'S LOST *ALL* MOTION TO THE LEFT SIDE OF HIS *BODY*.

YOU WORKED UNDER HIM?

WE SPOKE QUITE OFTEN WHILE I WAS IN WASHINGTON, BUT THE POSTING WASN'T DIRECTLY TASKED TO *SIS*.

JIC LIAISON, WITH INPUT, OF COURSE, BUT MOSTLY COMMUNICATING THROUGH THE *FCO* RATHER THAN DIRECT TO *SIS*.

WHAT DID YOU THINK OF HIM?

ONE *NEVER* DOUBTED HIS PASSION OR *LOYALTY* TO THE *SERVICE*.

AH, I *SEE*.

NO, NO ONE *EVER* DOUBTED SIR WILSON ABOUT *THAT*, I AGREE.

THE *WORLD* KEEPS SHIFTING ON US, FRANCES. AND THE SERVICE IS *STRUGGLING* TO KEEP UP.

THIS *THING* IN IRAQ, THE REFOCUSING ON *UBL* AND HIS *ILK*, THE ENDLESS INQUIRIES INTO OFF-SHORE ACCOUNTS AND WIRE-TRANSFERS...

...FOR *ALL* THAT SIR WILSON WAS A *GIFTED* SPYMASTER, THERE ARE A *NUMBER* OF MY PEERS IN WHITEHALL WHO FEEL THAT HE NEVER TRULY *GRASPED* THE MORE...NUANCED ELEMENTS OF ALLIED COOPERATION.

THERE ARE MANY WHO FEEL A *MORE* DIPLOMATIC APPROACH TO INTELLIGENCE WOULD HAVE SUITED US BETTER. *NEVER* BEEN ONE OF *YOUR* PROBLEMS, THOUGH, HAS IT, FRANCES?

WHO ELSE IS ON THE *SHORT-LIST*?

DONALD WELDON, OF COURSE, BUT MORE OUT OF *COURTESY* THAN ANYTHING ELSE. DENNIS RAMSEY AT THE *MOD*, BUT HE'S CLEARLY ON THE *OUTSIDE*, AS WELL, AND HAS *NO* EXPERIENCE IN *S/S*.

THE COMMITTEE IS STILL PUTTING TOGETHER *NAMES*.

MY *MINISTER* HAS BEEN *QUITE* CLEAR, FRANCES. HE WANTS A *RECOMMENDATION* BEFORE THE PRIME MINISTER BY THE END OF THE *WEEK*.

ONE THAT WILL WIN APPROVAL FOR *IMMEDIATE* APPOINTMENT. ONE THAT WILL TAKE THE SERVICE IN THE *RIGHT* DIRECTION.

AS I STATED *BEFORE*, WALTER, I HAVE VERY *SPECIFIC* IDEAS WITH REGARDS TO THE DIRECTION OF THE SERVICE.

WE'VE RELIED ON *ELINT* FOR TOO LONG, AND THEN USED SPECIAL OPERATIONS AS A STOP-GAP IN *CRISIS* SITUATIONS.

AND WHILE *ELINT* HAS ITS *PLACE*, WE DO OURSELVES MORE HARM THAN GOOD IF WE CANNOT SUPPLEMENT OUR INTELLIGENCE WITH *SOLID HUMINT* SOURCES.

STATIONS *MUST* EXIST TO *SERVE* THE INTELLIGENCE DIRECTORATES. OPERATIONAL CONCERNS BY DESIGN WOULD BE *SECONDARY* TO THAT GOAL.

THEIR FOCUS SHOULD BE LIMITED TO EITHER THE PRODUCTION AND PROCUREMENT OF HIGH-GRADE INTELLIGENCE, OR TO THE MAINTENANCE OF THOSE *LONG-TERM* OPERATIONS THAT ARE OUR *BREAD* AND *BUTTER*.

AND SIR WILSON WAS TOO PERMISSIVE IN THE FORMER?

SIR WILSON RELIED ON OPS TO THE EXCLUSION OF ALL ELSE, IN MY OPINION--AND IN THE OPINIONS OF *OTHERS* ON THE *JIC*, I SHOULD ADD.

THIS IS NOT INTENDED AS A *SLIGHT* OF SIR WILSON, WALTER, PLEASE UNDERSTAND...

...RATHER IT'S A *COMMENT* ON PAUL CROCKER AND HIS UNIQUE *ARROGANCE*. SOMETHING I WILL PUT A *QUICK* STOP TO, SHOULD THE OPPORTUNITY PRESENT ITSELF.

I WASN'T *AWARE* THAT YOU *KNEW* CROCKER.

OH, I *KNOW* HIM, WALTER...

...AND *HE* KNOWS *ME*....

PASSIVE *SURVEILLANCE,* THEN?

HMM?

PASSIVE SURVEILLANCE...

...YOU'VE BEEN *STARING* OUT THAT WINDOW FOR THE LAST *HOUR.*

AND HOPING THAT *YOU* WOULD *NOTICE* AND GIVE ME *GRIEF* FOR IT.

YOU HAVE ANY *OTHER* OBSERVATIONS YOU'D CARE TO MAKE, *KATE?*

JUST THE *ONE.*

DO YOU *SPEAK* TO YOUR *WIFE* THIS WAY? IF SO, IT'S A *WONDER* YOU'RE *STILL* MARRIED.

YES, WELL, KATE, YOU'RE NOT *MY* WIFE.

AND I THANK CHRIST FOR *THAT* FACT *EVERY* DAY.

WAIT A MINUTE--

--DID YOU CONTACT THE SCHOOL?

YES, SIR.

AND?

MISTER CHESTER SAYS THERE'S *NO ONE* IN THE CURRENT CLASS APPROPRIATE FOR SPECIAL OPERATIONS.

NO, OF *COURSE* HE'D SAY *THAT*, WOULDN'T HE?

AND WHERE THE HELL *ARE* THE MINDERS?

WALLACE WENT TO BATH TO SPEAK TO BUTLER'S *SISTER*.

CHACE CALLED IN *SICK*.

SICK. IS *THAT* WHAT SHE'S CALLING IT?

GO AWAY.

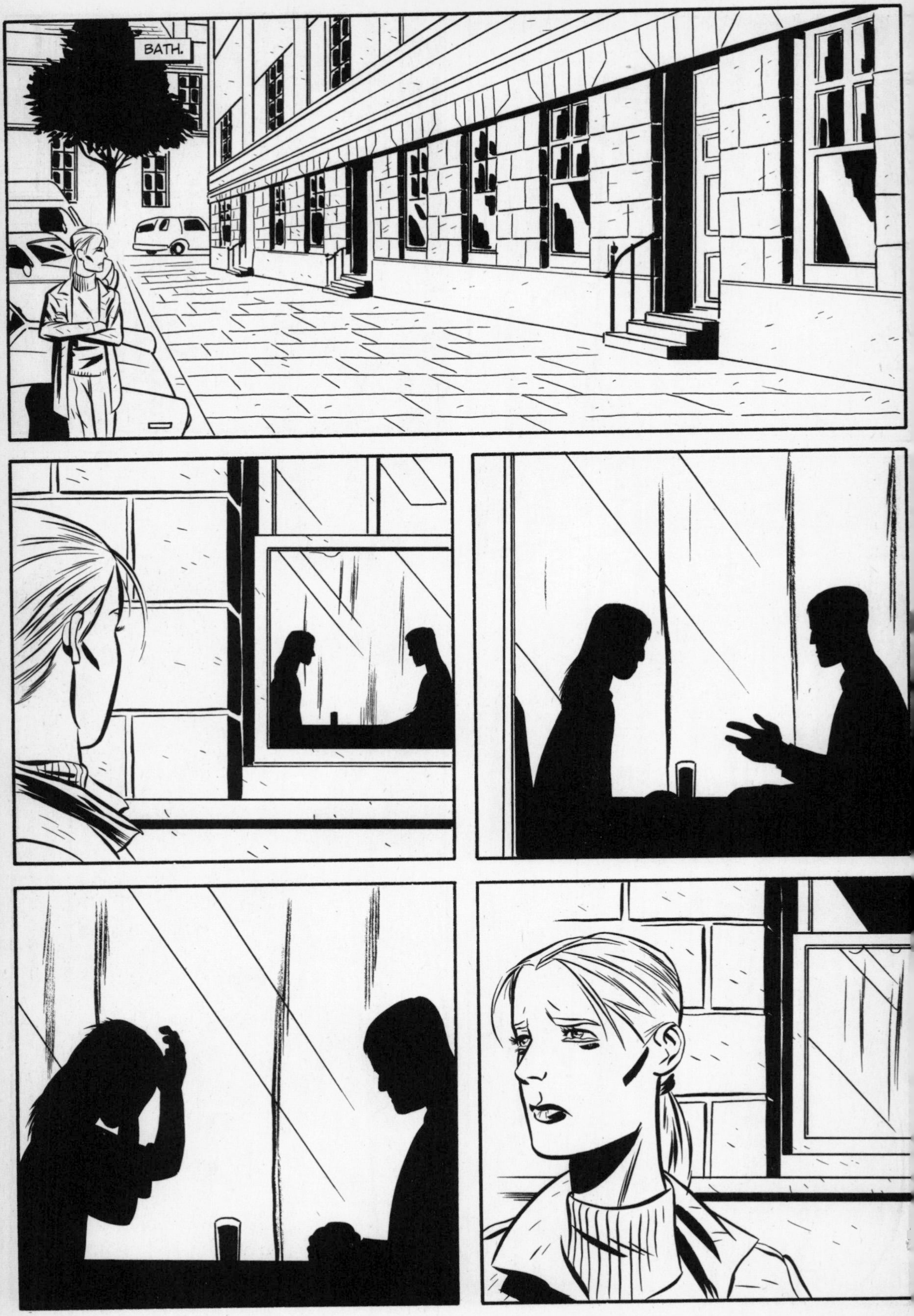
BATH.

YOU SEE A *PUB* ON THE WAY UP HERE?

I SAW *THREE* PUBS.

LET'S GET PISSED.

HAD TO BE *DONE,* TOM.

AND THAT MAKES IT *BETTER* HOW, EXACTLY?

IT DOESN'T.

I DON'T *NEED* YOUR APPROVAL, PAUL. IT'S A *RECOMMENDATION* TO THE *FCO*, AND IT WAS SENT DOWN TO YOU AND SIMON AS A *COURTESY*, NOTHING MORE.

YOU ASKED FOR MY OPINION, SIR.

I *DID*, YES. WE HAVE TO CUT *COSTS* SOMEWHERE.

NOT AT THE STATION LEVEL.

WHERE ELSE-- WE'VE CUT BACK ON *STATION* FINANCING *SIX TIMES* IN THE LAST *EIGHTEEN* MONTHS, SIR.

WE CUT BACK ANY *FURTHER*, BANGKOK WILL BE USING TWO EMPTY *CANS* AND A *BIT OF TWINE* FOR THEIR *COMS*.

CUTS *MUST* BE *MADE*-- NOT IN *OPS*.

HMG MUST BE MADE TO UNDERSTAND THAT THEY *CANNOT* DEMAND ACCURATE INTEL FROM US AT ONE TURN WHILST *TYING* OUR *HANDS* BEHIND OUR BACK AT THE *NEXT*.

THEY'RE ASKING US TO *FIGHT* A *WAR*, AND THEY'RE *PICKING* OUR POCKETS AS WE *MARCH* TO THE FIELD.

AND WHEN *YOU* PUT FORWARD *PROPOSALS* LIKE THIS ONE, SIR, IT ONLY MAKES MATTERS *WORSE*.

SO WHERE ARE THE CUTS TO COME FROM, PAUL?

THEY SHOULDN'T COME FROM *ANYWHERE*. THEY SHOULD BE *DOUBLING* OUR BUDGET, THAT'S WHAT THEY *SHOULD* BE DOING.

I'LL BE SURE TO TELL THEM *THAT.*

SEE THAT YOU DO.

WAS THERE SOMETHING *ELSE,* PAUL?

YES, SIR. HAVE YOU HEARD ANYTHING ABOUT SIR MICHAEL?

NOTHING THAT YOU HAVEN'T *ALREADY.* THE *STROKE* TOOK HIS *LEFT* SIDE. HE WON'T BE COMING BACK.

IT'S BEEN A *WEEK* AND THE *PM* HASN'T ANNOUNCED A *REPLACEMENT.*

PRESUMABLY, THEY'RE STILL *VETTING.*

BUT YOU'VE *SPOKEN* TO WALTER SECCOMBE.

HAD *LUNCH* AT HIS CLUB, IN FACT.

YOU'RE IN *CONSIDERATION?*

I CAN'T COMMENT, PAUL. NOW, DON'T YOU HAVE *SOMETHING* YOU SHOULD BE *DOING?*

IT'S ONLY MY *SECOND*, AND I'M NOT *DONE* YET, SO I'D SAY I'M *STILL* SOBER.

I AM *FORCED* TO *CONCLUDE* THAT I *AM*, IN FACT, *SERIOUS*.

WHAT'S HER *NAME*?

THERE DOESN'T HAVE TO BE A *BIRD* BEHIND IT, TARA. I *AM* CAPABLE OF REACHING MY *OWN* CONCLUSIONS WITHOUT SEX OBFUSCATING MY THOUGHTS.

OH, YOU? YOU'RE A *DIRTY* OLD MAN, TOM! YOU GET *DIZZY* PASSING THE UNMENTIONABLES IN MARKS AND SPARKS.

...COULD BE *MY* TURN TO SEND THE BAGS DOWN TO THE *LOBBY* AND CHECK OUT SOON ENOUGH.

YOU CAN *RUN* THE SECTION. YOU'D BE *DAMN* GOOD AT IT.

I DON'T *WANT* IT.

I'VE BEEN THINKING ABOUT IT FOR A *WHILE* NOW.

HOW LONG IS A *WHILE*?

FIVE, SIX MONTHS. SINCE ED DIED. I DON'T *KNOW*, TARA.

YOU *CAN'T* BE SERIOUS.

CAN'T I? I *THINK* I CAN.

THEY SPRAY *PERFUME* IN THERE, I'M SURE OF IT.

NO, I'M *SERIOUS*, TARA.

LAW OF *AVERAGES*, ISN'T IT? AND I'VE GOT *SEVEN* YEARS IN, NOW...

YES YOU *DO*. YOU WANT CROCKER'S *JOB*.

I'LL GET TWO *MORE*, SHALL I?

WHAT HAVE YOU *HEARD*?

I WAS ABOUT TO ASK YOU THE *SAME* THING.

YOU THINK THE *CIA* HAS INPUT INTO THE APPOINTMENT OF A NEW *C*?

NO, BUT I KNOW HOW THE *U.S.* LIKES TO FEEL *INVOLVED*, ANGELA.

IT MAKES US FEEL *USEFUL*. ALL I KNOW IS THAT THE *PM* IS LOOKING FOR A *NAME* BY THE END OF THE *WEEK*.

YES, WELL, THAT'S *COMMON* KNOWLEDGE, ISN'T IT?

ALL RIGHT, THEN, SMART-ASS. YOU *TELL* ME.

THE *PUS* AT THE *FCO* HAS BEEN *VETTING* NAMES. TOOK WELDON TO *LUNCH* YESTERDAY, AT HIS *CLUB*.

YOU'RE *NOT* SERIOUS.

YOU THINK I WOULD *JOKE* ABOUT THAT?

DONALD WELDON AS *CHIEF* OF SIS. SHOOT ME *NOW*.

YOU'LL HAVE TO *JOIN* THE *QUEUE.*

NO, HE *WON'T* GET IT. HE HAS THE *YEARS,* BUT NOT THE *POLITICS.*

THEN SOMEONE FROM THE *JIC* OR *SIS* IN WHITEHALL.

YES, PROBABLY *BOTH.*

YOU DON'T HAVE *STAPLERS* IN YOUR OFFICE?

NO, WE *DO.* OURS JUST DON'T SAY "PROPERTY OF THE *CIA*" ON THEM.

CUTS DOWN ON *OFFICE* THEFT.

NO DOUBT. MORE I THINK ABOUT IT, THE MORE I THINK IT'LL *HAVE* TO BE *SIS* POSTED TO THE *JIC,* AND FAIRLY *SENIOR* IN THE POSITION, AT THAT.

A POST ON THE JOINT INTELLIGENCE COMMITTEE WOULD BE *MORE* POLITICAL, THAT'S FOR SURE.

AND GIVEN THE *CURRENT* CLIMATE, THE *PM* WILL WANT SOMEONE WITH *ESTABLISHED* TIES TO WASHINGTON, SOMEONE WHO GETS ON WITH YOUR *LOT.*

THEN MAYBE WE'LL *LUCK* OUT...

...GET A *C* WHO DOESN'T MIND THE FACT THAT WE'RE ALL *COZY* BENEATH THE *SHEETS* TOGETHER.

YOU SPEND *FAR* TOO MUCH TIME THINKING ABOUT *SEX,* YOU KNOW THAT?

YEAH, AND NOT *ENOUGH* TIME ACTUALLY *DOING* ANYTHING TO *GET* SOME.

THEY *NEVER* TOLD US IT WOULD BE *THIS* VIOLENT...

...I MEAN, I CAN *STILL* HEAR JIM CHESTER TELLING ME THAT MINDERS *RARELY* KILL OR *GET* KILLED.

HE'S NOT *WRONG*, YOU KNOW. ED WENT BECAUSE IT WAS HIS *TIME*.

IT'S *POOR* BRIAN WHO GOT ONE OF THE "TO WHOM IT MAY CONCERNS."

YOU *BELIEVE* THE STORY ABOUT AN *ANEURYSM*?

CHRIST, YOU'RE A *SUSPICIOUS* BAG, AREN'T YOU?

I DON'T KNOW. IT'S JUST...IT'S SUCH A FUCKING *PEDESTRIAN* WAY TO DIE.

HE'S JAMES FUCKING BOND, YOU DON'T *EXPECT* HIM TO SNUFF IT BECAUSE HE KEPT *IGNORING* A BLOODY *HEADACHE*.

AT LEAST, *I* DIDN'T.

YOU DIDN'T HAVE TO *COME* WITH ME TODAY, YOU KNOW.

IT WAS A *CONDOLENCE* CALL, NOTHING MORE.

I WAS IN THE FUCKING CAR *NEXT* TO BRIAN WHEN HE *DIED*.

I SHOULD HAVE COME *INSIDE*, SPOKEN TO HIS *SISTER*.

AND SAID *WHAT?* THE FCO HAD *ALREADY* INFORMED HER. IF YOU HAD COME IN, SHE'D HAVE WONDERED WHY THERE WERE *TWO* OF US.

WOULD HAVE LED TO *UNCOMFORTABLE* QUESTIONS.

THEY *DIDN'T TELL* HER?

WHAT WERE THEY GOING TO SAY? I'M SORRY, MISS, YOUR BROTHER WAS MURDERED WHILST ENGAGED IN A COVERT OPERATION IN GEORGIA?

THEY GAVE HER SOME RUBBISH ABOUT BRIAN BEING A *COURIER*, HIS *PLANE* GOING DOWN IN THE *GULF*.

EXPLAINS WHY THERE'S NO *BODY* FOR THE *FUNERAL*.

JESUS, TOM.

NOW YOU'RE MAKING *ME* WANT TO *QUIT*, TOO.

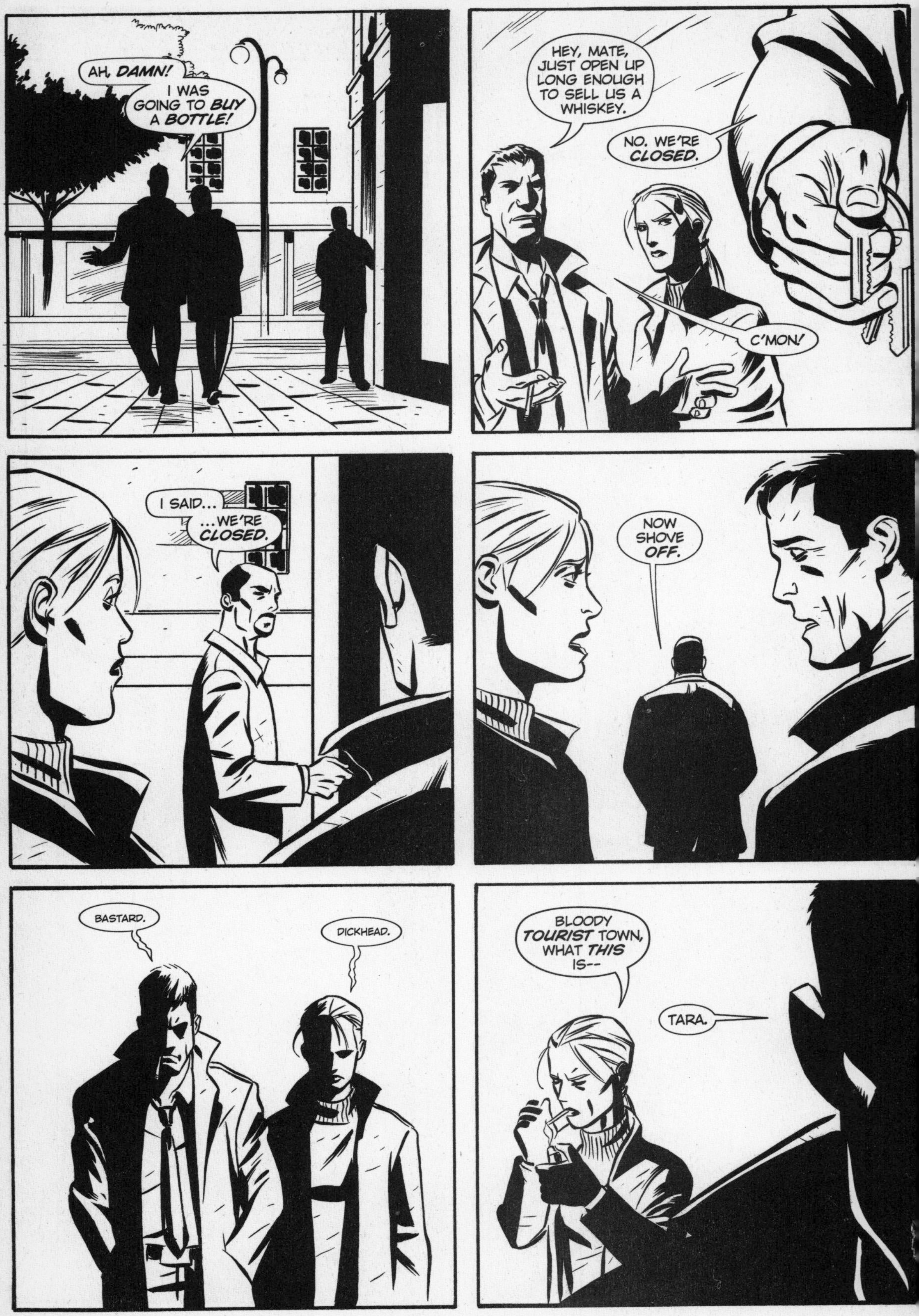
AH, DAMN!
I WAS GOING TO BUY A BOTTLE!
HEY, MATE, JUST OPEN UP LONG ENOUGH TO SELL US A WHISKEY.
NO. WE'RE CLOSED.
C'MON!
I SAID...
...WE'RE CLOSED.
NOW SHOVE OFF.
BASTARD.
DICKHEAD.
BLOODY TOURIST TOWN, WHAT THIS IS--
TARA.

TAKE A LOOK, EH?

NOT FAIR, THAT'S WHAT THIS IS.

AFTER ALL *WE* DO FOR THIS COUNTRY, AND THEY STILL CAN'T BE *BOTHERED* TO SELL US A *DRINK* WHEN WE *NEED* ONE.

THAT'S *NOT BLOODY RIGHT*.

NO, IT BLOODY WELL ISN'T.

RIGHT.

RIGHT.

WAIT FOR ME.

RIGHT.

WHAT'S *THAT*?

TIRE IRON.

OH.

TOM...?

KSSSSSSSH

YES, LOVE?

...NEVER MIND.

BEST START THE *CAR*, THEN.

RIGHT.

OH, WAIT!

HMM?

HOLD ON...

...PAY FOR THE *DAMAGES*.

OH, RIGHT! BLOODY BRILLIANT, THAT!

THINK I'VE GOT 'ROUND *SIXTY*.

HURRY, TOM!

RIGHT, RIGHT, HURRY, YES...

...JUST COMING.

DREET DREET

PA TO D. OPS. ...NO, HE'S *FREE* AFTER ELEVEN-THIRTY...

...I'LL CHECK WITH HIM AND GET BACK TO YOU.

CHECK WITH ME ABOUT *WHAT?*

I SHOULD HAVE *KNOWN* YOU WERE HERE ALREADY. WHAT TIME DID YOU GET IN?

SIX. WHO WAS THAT?

THAT WAS SIR WALTER SECCOMBE'S *PERSONAL* SECRETARY.

EXPRESSING THE *PUS'S DESIRE* TO *LUNCH* WITH YOU AT HIS *CLUB.*

SHALL I RING BACK AND *EXPRESS* YOUR *REGRETS?*

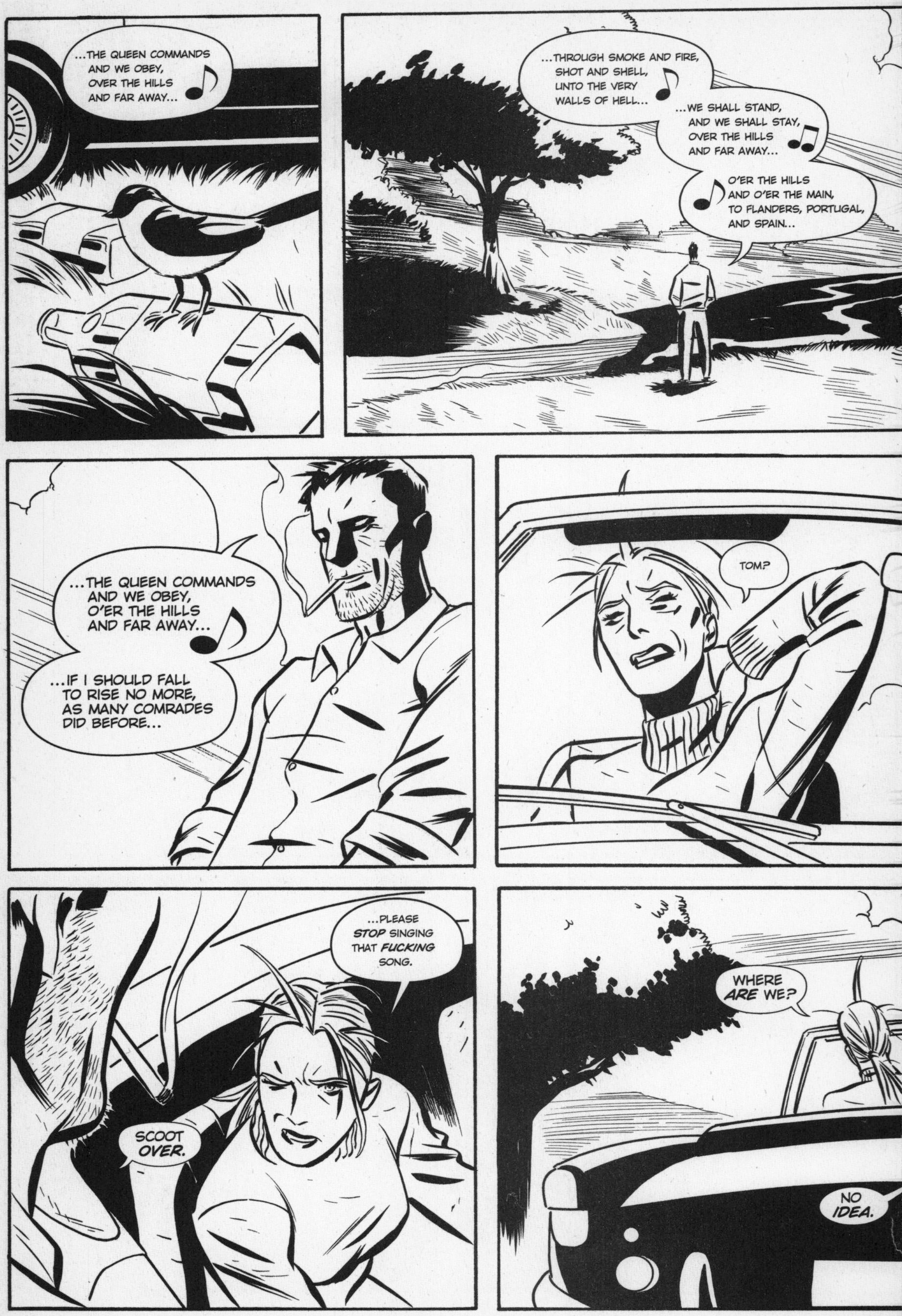

...THE QUEEN COMMANDS AND WE OBEY, OVER THE HILLS AND FAR AWAY...
...THROUGH SMOKE AND FIRE, SHOT AND SHELL, UNTO THE VERY WALLS OF HELL...
...WE SHALL STAND, AND WE SHALL STAY, OVER THE HILLS AND FAR AWAY...
O'ER THE HILLS AND O'ER THE MAIN, TO FLANDERS, PORTUGAL, AND SPAIN...
...THE QUEEN COMMANDS AND WE OBEY, O'ER THE HILLS AND FAR AWAY...
...IF I SHOULD FALL TO RISE NO MORE, AS MANY COMRADES DID BEFORE...
TOM?
...PLEASE STOP SINGING THAT FUCKING SONG.
SCOOT OVER.
WHERE ARE WE?
NO IDEA.

...THEN ASK THE FIFE AND DRUM TO PLAY, OVER THE HILLS AND FAR AWAY...

YES, LOVE?

IN THE *NAME* OF *ALL* THAT IS *HOLY*...

TOM? WHY DON'T I HAVE ANY *MONEY*?

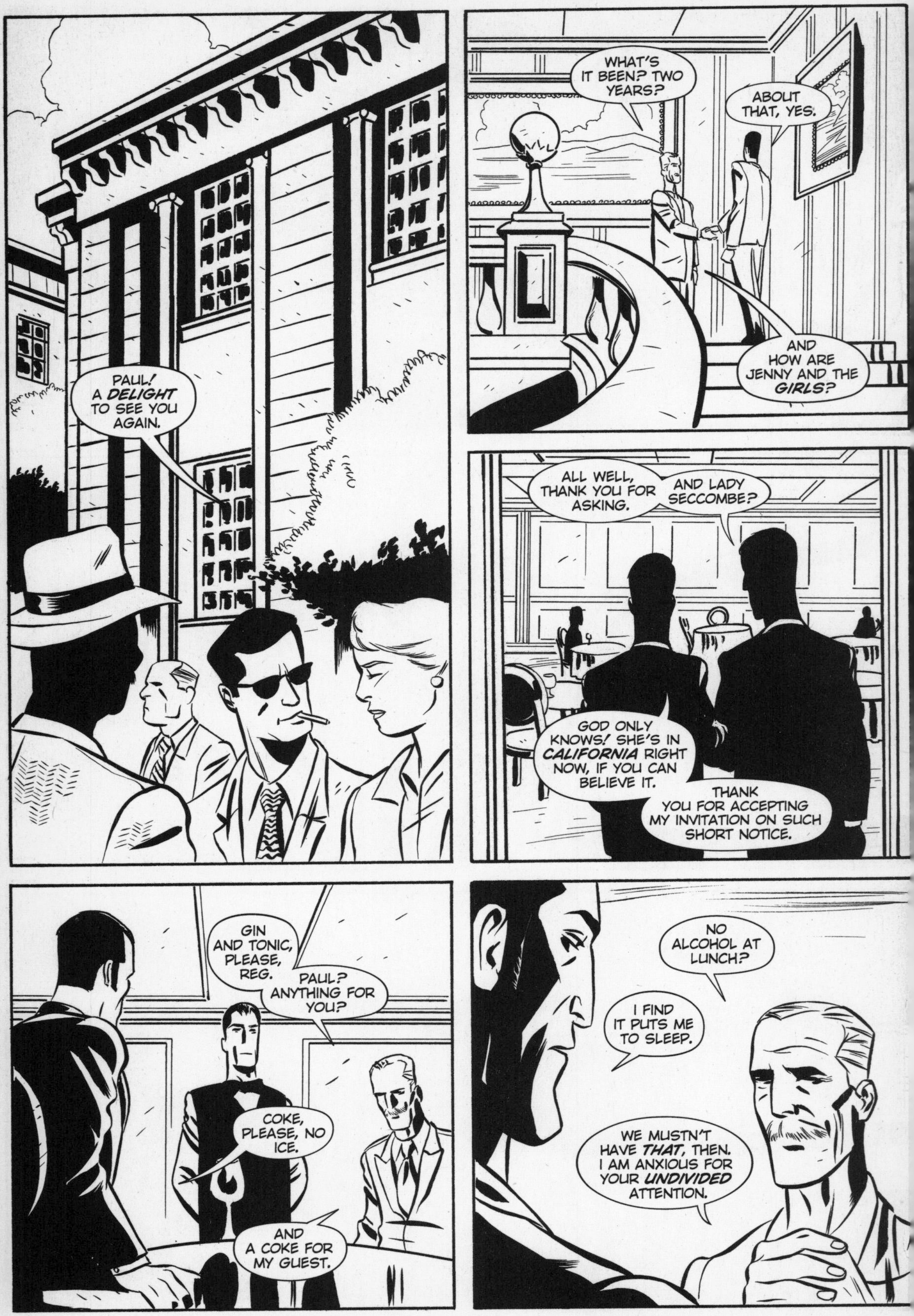
PAUL! A DELIGHT TO SEE YOU AGAIN.
WHAT'S IT BEEN? TWO YEARS?
ABOUT THAT, YES.
AND HOW ARE JENNY AND THE GIRLS?
ALL WELL, THANK YOU FOR ASKING.
AND LADY SECCOMBE?
GOD ONLY KNOWS! SHE'S IN CALIFORNIA RIGHT NOW, IF YOU CAN BELIEVE IT.
THANK YOU FOR ACCEPTING MY INVITATION ON SUCH SHORT NOTICE.
GIN AND TONIC, PLEASE, REG.
PAUL? ANYTHING FOR YOU?
COKE, PLEASE, NO ICE.
AND A COKE FOR MY GUEST.
NO ALCOHOL AT LUNCH?
I FIND IT PUTS ME TO SLEEP.
WE MUSTN'T HAVE THAT, THEN. I AM ANXIOUS FOR YOUR UNDIVIDED ATTENTION.

THE INVITATION ALONE GUARANTEED THAT. I WAS MORE THAN A LITTLE SURPRISED.

YOU WANT TO KNOW WHAT I'M AFTER.

OF COURSE.

WHO SAYS I'M AFTER ANYTHING, PAUL?

THE FACT THAT THE PUS AT THE FCO DOES NOT LUNCH WITH THE OPS DIRECTOR OF SIS, FOR A START. AND AT HIS CLUB? TONGUES WILL BE WAGGING.

LET THEM WAG. THE OWNERS OF THOSE TONGUES COULD USE A LITTLE EXERCISE.

AH, SO THERE IS LAUGHTER IN YOU AFTER ALL. ALL RUMORS TO THE CONTRARY NOTWITHSTANDING.

WHAT DO YOU WANT, SIR WALTER?

WELL, I SHOULD THINK IT'S OBVIOUS, SHOULDN'T YOU?

JUST AS OBVIOUS AS THE FACT THAT I'M NOT EVEN IN CONSIDERATION FOR THE VACANCY YOU'RE WORKING TO FILL.

THAT DISTRESSES YOU?

IN ANOTHER TEN YEARS IT MIGHT. I DON'T HAVE SENIORITY.

NOR THE POLITICS, I'M AFRAID. BUT I CAN CERTAINLY HELP YOU WITH THE LATTER, AND IN SO DOING, OFFER YOU A LEG UP ON THE FORMER.

ARE YOU *OFFERING* TO TAKE ME UNDER YOUR *WING?*

YOU COULD DO FAR *WORSE* THAN AN *ALLY* IN THE *FCO,* PAUL.

IN EXCHANGE FOR *WHAT?*

COME MONDAY, FRANCES BARCLAY WILL BE YOUR *NEW C.* AND I HAVE IT ON *VERY* GOOD AUTHORITY THAT, COME TUESDAY, YOU'LL BE SETTING UP STATION IN GREENLAND.

LET'S ORDER LUNCH, PAUL.

AND *AFTERWARDS,* WE CAN DISCUSS WHAT *I* CAN DO FOR *YOU...*

...AND WHAT *YOU* CAN DO FOR *ME....*

CHAPTER 2

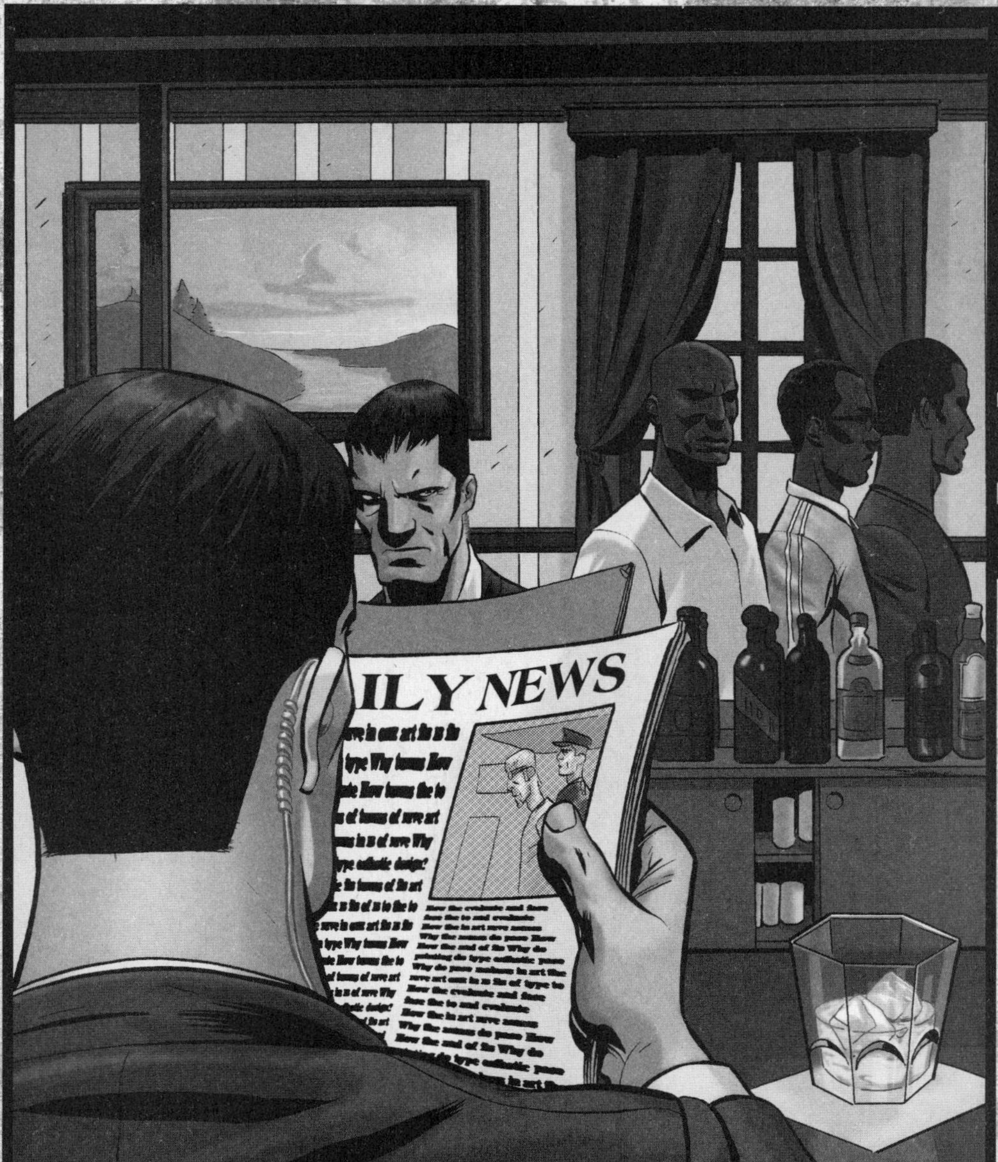
ILY NEWS

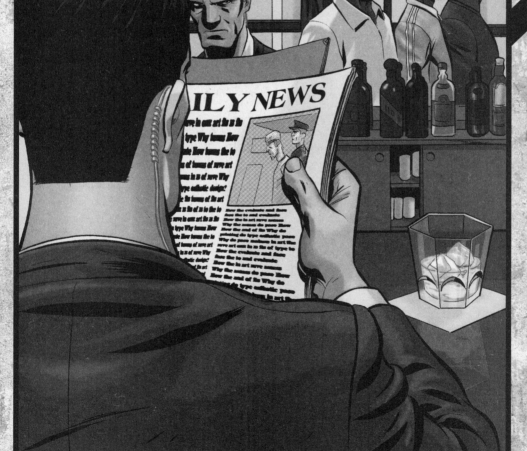

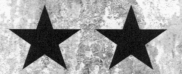

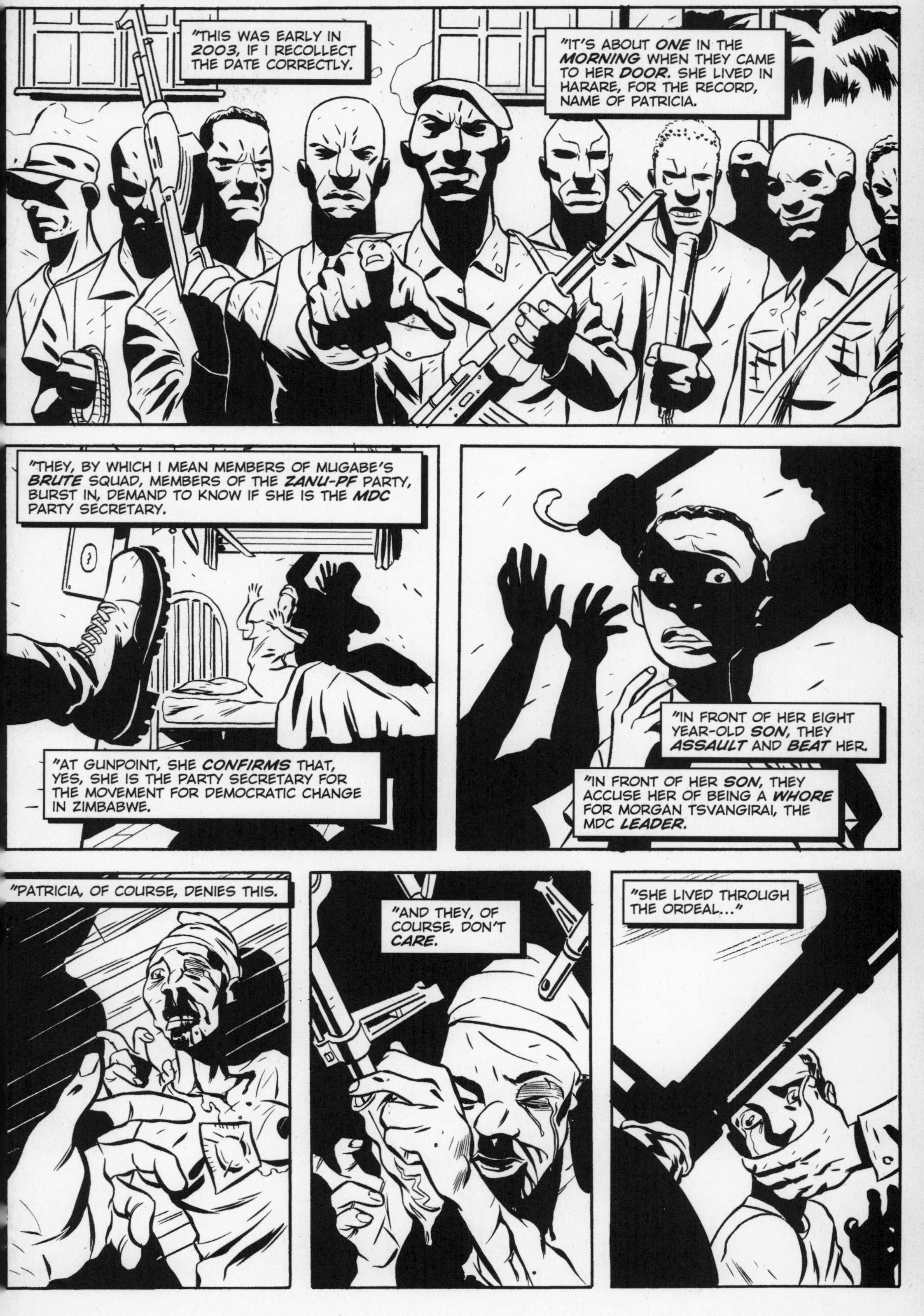
"THIS WAS EARLY IN 2003, IF I RECOLLECT THE DATE CORRECTLY.
"IT'S ABOUT ONE IN THE MORNING WHEN THEY CAME TO HER DOOR. SHE LIVED IN HARARE, FOR THE RECORD, NAME OF PATRICIA.
"THEY, BY WHICH I MEAN MEMBERS OF MUGABE'S BRUTE SQUAD, MEMBERS OF THE ZANU-PF PARTY, BURST IN, DEMAND TO KNOW IF SHE IS THE MDC PARTY SECRETARY.
"AT GUNPOINT, SHE CONFIRMS THAT, YES, SHE IS THE PARTY SECRETARY FOR THE MOVEMENT FOR DEMOCRATIC CHANGE IN ZIMBABWE.
"IN FRONT OF HER EIGHT YEAR-OLD SON, THEY ASSAULT AND BEAT HER.
"IN FRONT OF HER SON, THEY ACCUSE HER OF BEING A WHORE FOR MORGAN TSVANGIRAI, THE MDC LEADER.
"PATRICIA, OF COURSE, DENIES THIS.
"AND THEY, OF COURSE, DON'T CARE.
"SHE LIVED THROUGH THE ORDEAL..."

...INCLUDING FURTHER DEGRADATION AND BRUTALITY, SUCH AS BEING FORCED TO DRINK HER SON'S *URINE*.

I'VE *READ* THE REPORTS.

OF COURSE YOU HAVE, PAUL.

ARE YOU *FINISHED*? DO YOU NEED TO GET BACK TO THE OFFICE?

I SHOULD START HEADING BACK, YES.

I'LL WALK YOU OUT.

I'VE FELT FOR A VERY LONG TIME THAT THE GOVERNMENT SHOULD BE PLAYING A *LARGER* PART IN THE FUTURE OF ZIMBABWE, PAUL.

WE *DID* CREATE THE *MESS*, AFTER ALL.

HOW *LARGE* A PART, EXACTLY, SIR WALTER?

FRANCES BARCLAY DOESN'T *FRIGHTEN* ME.

INDEED? WELL, I *DOUBT* MUCH *DOES*. BUT *YOU* FRIGHTEN *HIM*, AND THAT'S WHY HE'LL DO *EVERYTHING* HE CAN TO REMOVE YOU AS D-OPS.

IT DOESN'T HELP THAT BARCLAY BELIEVES THAT OPERATIONS HAS *NO* DEMONSTRABLE BENEFIT TO THE GOVERNMENT. A *VIEW* THAT *OTHERS* IN WHITEHALL SHARE, I HASTEN TO ADD.

THEY'RE *FOOLS*.

AND THERE'S THAT *LACK OF TACT* AGAIN.

NOW, IF SIS WERE TO *PROVE* TO HMG THE *VALUE* OF THE OPS DIRECTORATE, YOU'D BE IN A *MUCH* STRONGER POSITION BOTH WITH REGARD TO BARCLAY AND TO THE *REST* OF WHITEHALL.

AND YOU HAVE A *WAY* FOR ME TO *DO* THAT, DO YOU?

THEN WHY THE *BRIEFING?*

SO YOU *UNDERSTAND* THAT I HAVE READ THEM, *TOO.*

THAT *LACK* OF *TACT* IS *PRECISELY* WHY SIR FRANCES BARCLAY HAS MORE FRIENDS IN WHITEHALL THAN *YOU* DO.

AND *PRECISELY* WHY YOU NEED AN *ALLY*

IF SIS WERE TO DESIGN, IMPLEMENT, AND THEN EXECUTE THE *OVERTHROW* OF ROBERT MUGABE, THE OPS DIRECTORATE WOULD SUDDENLY FIND ITSELF *THICK* WITH *FRIENDS.*

AS A MATTER OF FACT, I DO.

AND THE D-OPS WHO *LEAD* THAT *CHARGE,* SO TO SPEAK, WOULD BE CONSIDERED *FAR* TOO VALUABLE TO *LOSE.*

HE MIGHT *EVEN* FIND HIMSELF NAMED *C,* ONE DAY.

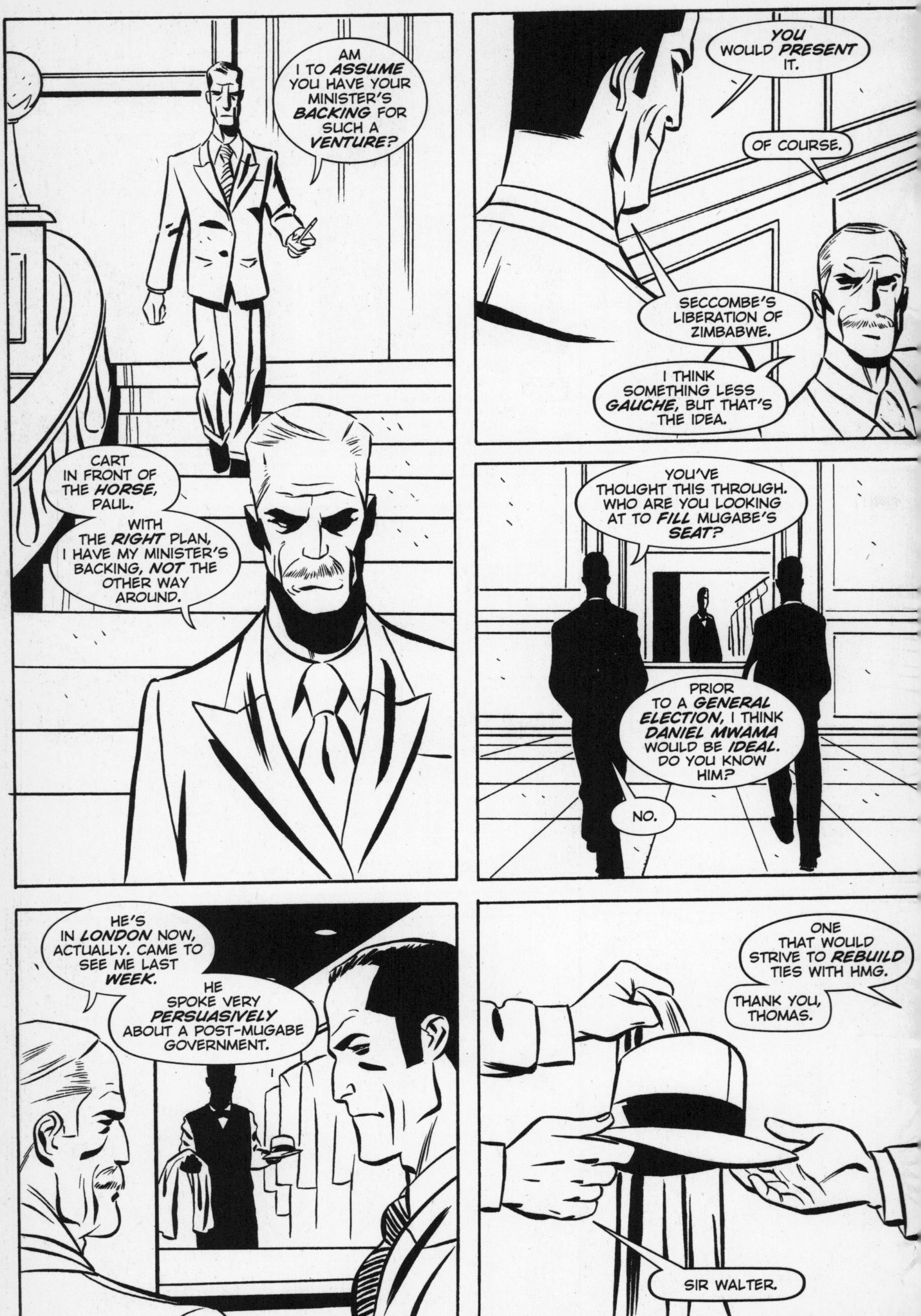
AM I TO ASSUME YOU HAVE YOUR MINISTER'S BACKING FOR SUCH A VENTURE?
CART IN FRONT OF THE HORSE, PAUL.
WITH THE RIGHT PLAN, I HAVE MY MINISTER'S BACKING, NOT THE OTHER WAY AROUND.
YOU WOULD PRESENT IT.
OF COURSE.
SECCOMBE'S LIBERATION OF ZIMBABWE.
I THINK SOMETHING LESS GAUCHE, BUT THAT'S THE IDEA.
YOU'VE THOUGHT THIS THROUGH. WHO ARE YOU LOOKING AT TO FILL MUGABE'S SEAT?
PRIOR TO A GENERAL ELECTION, I THINK DANIEL MWAMA WOULD BE IDEAL. DO YOU KNOW HIM?
NO.
HE'S IN LONDON NOW, ACTUALLY. CAME TO SEE ME LAST WEEK.
HE SPOKE VERY PERSUASIVELY ABOUT A POST-MUGABE GOVERNMENT.
ONE THAT WOULD STRIVE TO REBUILD TIES WITH HMG.
THANK YOU, THOMAS.
SIR WALTER.

HOW LONG WILL YOU *NEED*?

A COUPLE OF MONTHS.

YOU HAVE UNTIL MONDAY.

THAT'S *NOT* A LOT OF *TIME*.

NO, BUT EVEN WITHOUT BARCLAY IN THE *EQUATION* I'D WANT IT PUT TOGETHER *QUICKLY*.

I DON'T WANT MWAMA GOING TO THE *CIA*, YOU UNDERSTAND.

THE CURRENT PRESIDENT'S *INTEREST* IN AFRICA IS CONFINED *SOLELY* TO *IMAGE-BUILDING*. THEY'D *NEVER* UNDERTAKE ANYTHING SO RISKY.

NONETHELESS.

IT NEEDN'T BE THE *FINAL* DRAFT, JUST A *STRONG* INITIAL PROPOSAL.

WE'LL HAVE TO CHECK MWAMA *FIRST*.

WHAT ON EARTH FOR?

TO SEE THAT HE'S ON THE *LEVEL*, FOR A START. MWAMA COULD BE A MUGABE *PLANT*, FOR ALL WE KNOW.

TO WHAT *END*?

NO IDEA. BUT UNTIL WE KNOW *MORE* ABOUT MWAMA, IT WOULD BE *FOOLISH* TO START PLANNING A *COUP*.

DOES HE HAVE MDC BACKING, FOR INSTANCE? POPULAR SUPPORT? THERE ARE A LOT OF QUESTIONS.

AND *NOT A LOT* OF *TIME*.

YOU'VE MADE THAT *VERY* CLEAR.

MONDAY, PAUL.

I'LL LOOK FORWARD TO HEARING FROM YOU.

IS THERE *ANYTHING* I CAN GET YOU, SIR?

WE HAVE TEA AND COFFEE, IF YOU'D LIKE?

NO, THANK YOU.

WELCOME BACK, SIR. DID YOU HAVE A *PLEASANT* LUNCH?

DID SOMEONE *HIT* YOU IN THE *HEAD?* SINCE WHEN HAVE YOU *CARED* IF...

...RIGHT....

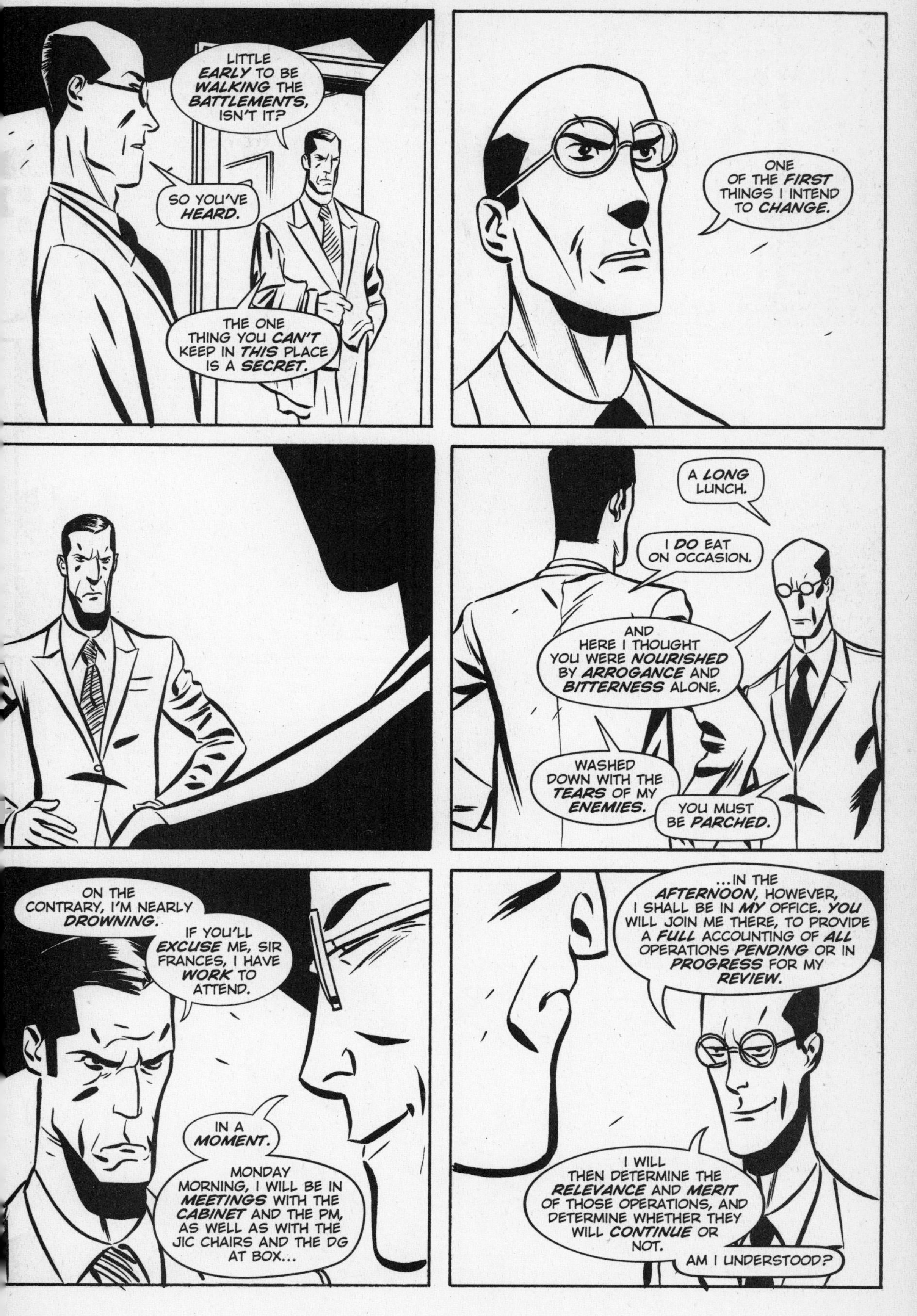
LITTLE EARLY TO BE WALKING THE BATTLEMENTS, ISN'T IT?
SO YOU'VE HEARD.
THE ONE THING YOU CAN'T KEEP IN THIS PLACE IS A SECRET.
ONE OF THE FIRST THINGS I INTEND TO CHANGE.
A LONG LUNCH.
I DO EAT ON OCCASION.
AND HERE I THOUGHT YOU WERE NOURISHED BY ARROGANCE AND BITTERNESS ALONE.
WASHED DOWN WITH THE TEARS OF MY ENEMIES.
YOU MUST BE PARCHED.
ON THE CONTRARY, I'M NEARLY DROWNING.
IF YOU'LL EXCUSE ME, SIR FRANCES, I HAVE WORK TO ATTEND.
IN A MOMENT.
MONDAY MORNING, I WILL BE IN MEETINGS WITH THE CABINET AND THE PM, AS WELL AS WITH THE JIC CHAIRS AND THE DG AT BOX...
...IN THE AFTERNOON, HOWEVER, I SHALL BE IN MY OFFICE. YOU WILL JOIN ME THERE, TO PROVIDE A FULL ACCOUNTING OF ALL OPERATIONS PENDING OR IN PROGRESS FOR MY REVIEW.
I WILL THEN DETERMINE THE RELEVANCE AND MERIT OF THOSE OPERATIONS, AND DETERMINE WHETHER THEY WILL CONTINUE OR NOT.
AM I UNDERSTOOD?

THIS SERVICE *CANNOT* SURVIVE WITHOUT AN OPERATIONS DIRECTORATE.

MEANING IT CANNOT *SURVIVE* WITHOUT *YOU*?

OF COURSE NOT...

...BUT REGARDLESS OF WHAT YOU FEEL ABOUT ME, OPERATIONS NEEDS A DIRECTOR WITH *FIELD* EXPERIENCE, NOT SOMEONE WHO SPENT HIS TOUR YEARS PLAYING *POLITICS*.

AND YOU FEEL I *LACK* THAT *EXPERTISE*?

BLUNTLY, YES, I DO.

SINCE WE'RE BEING *BLUNT*, PERHAPS YOU'LL ALLOW *ME*.

YOU THINK *PRAGUE* AND *LANDSLIDE* WERE *PERSONAL*, ALTHOUGH WE *NEVER* MET. YET *ANOTHER* EXAMPLE OF YOUR *STUNNING* ARROGANCE.

ALLOW ME TO *CLARIFY* FOR YOU...

...MY *OBLIGATION* WAS TO THE *STATION* AND ITS *NETWORK*, TO THE *AGENTS* IN THE FIELD WHO RELIED UPON US DAY-TO-DAY, YEAR AFTER *YEAR*.

NOT TO A MINDER WHO RODE IN LIKE A *COWBOY*, ONLY TO RIDE *OUT* AGAIN JUST AS QUICKLY.

THAT *SAME* OBLIGATION WILL GUIDE MY DECISIONS AS C.

AND THE MINDERS BE *DAMNED*.

THE MINDERS--AND *YOU*--HAVE YOUR *PLACE*. YOU *FOLLOW* POLICY, YOU DO *NOT* DICTATE IT.

ARE YOU *FINISHED*?

FOR *NOW*.

PLEASURE TO MEET YOU, KATE.

THANK YOU, SIR.

WHAT CAN I DO?

GET ON TO *SIMON*, TELL HIM I NEED *EVERYTHING* HE HAS ON A ZIMBABWEAN NATIONAL NAMED DANIEL MWAMA.

RIGHT.

AND THEN PULL THE *ABSTRACTS* FOR *EVERY* OPERATION AUTHORIZED OR *PENDING* AUTHORIZATION FOR THE NEXT SIX MONTHS.

OUR NEW C WANTS US TO *JUSTIFY* OUR *EXISTENCE* FOR HIM.

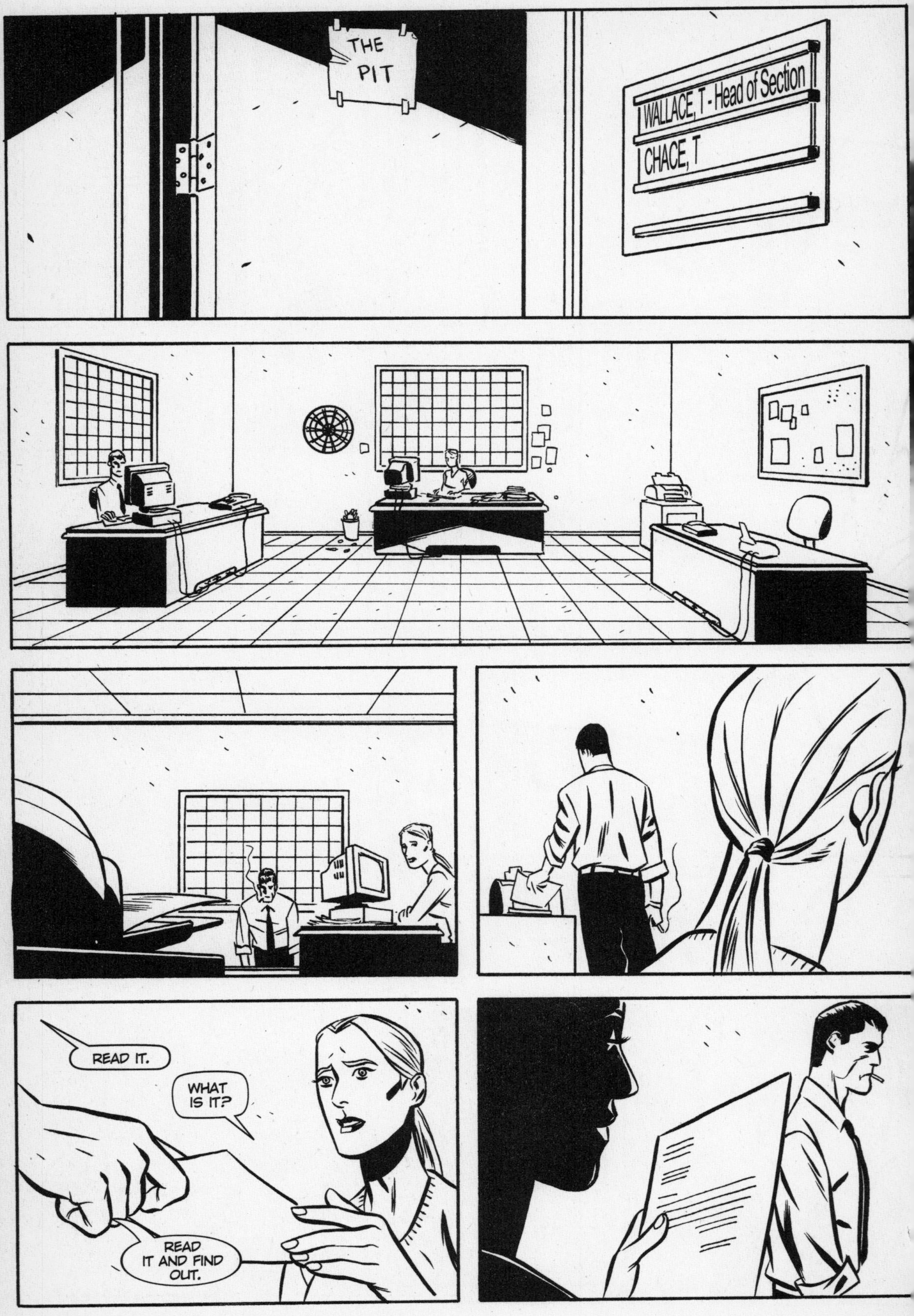
THE PIT
WALLACE, T - Head of Section
CHACE, T
READ IT.
WHAT IS IT?
READ IT AND FIND OUT.

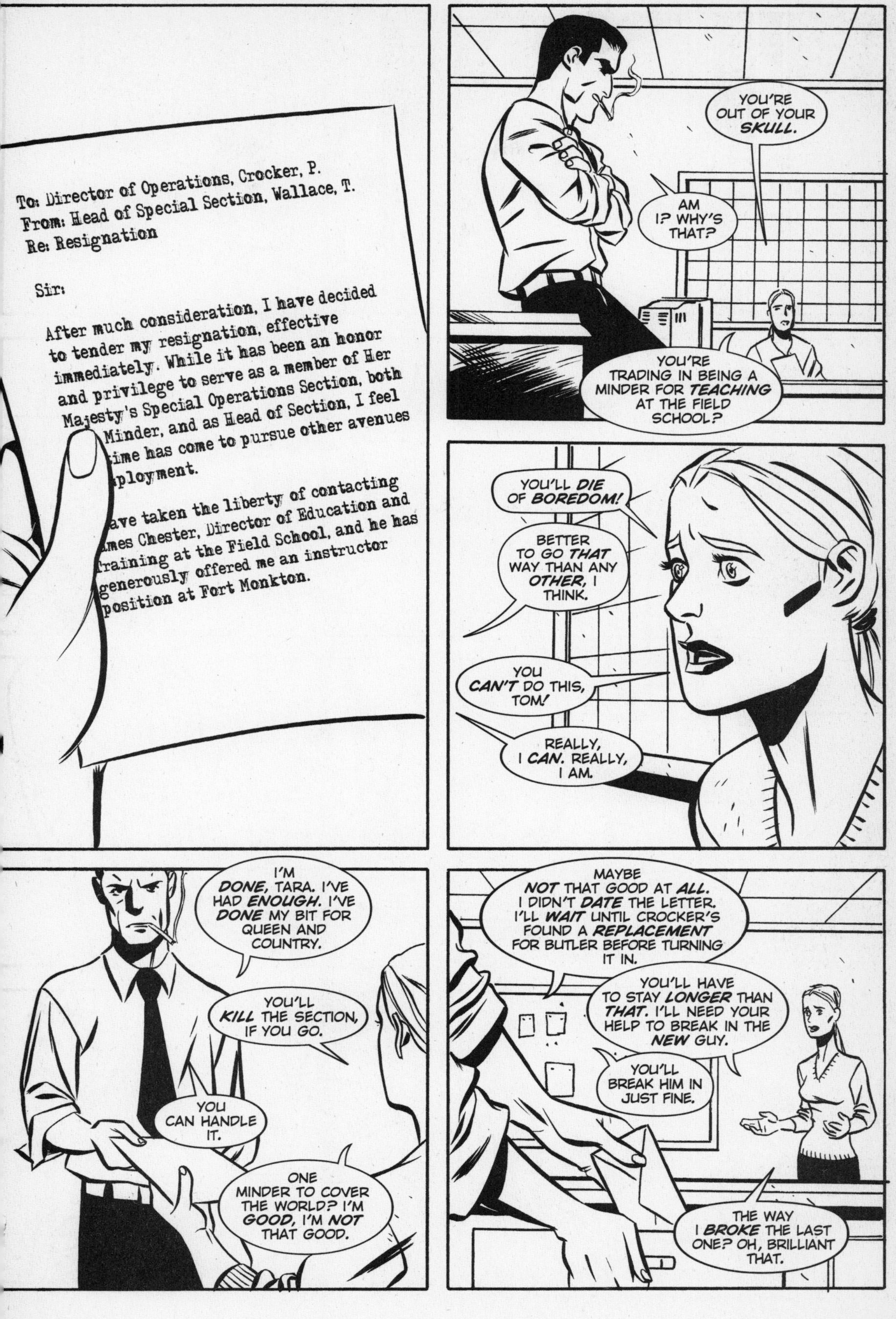
To: Director of Operations, Crocker, P.
From: Head of Special Section, Wallace, T.
Re: Resignation
Sir:
After much consideration, I have decided to tender my resignation, effective immediately. While it has been an honor and privilege to serve as a member of Her Majesty's Special Operations Section, both Minder, and as Head of Section, I feel time has come to pursue other avenues ployment.
ave taken the liberty of contacting mes Chester, Director of Education and Training at the Field School, and he has generously offered me an instructor position at Fort Monkton.
YOU'RE OUT OF YOUR SKULL.
AM I? WHY'S THAT?
YOU'RE TRADING IN BEING A MINDER FOR TEACHING AT THE FIELD SCHOOL?
YOU'LL DIE OF BOREDOM!
BETTER TO GO THAT WAY THAN ANY OTHER, I THINK.
YOU CAN'T DO THIS, TOM!
REALLY, I CAN. REALLY, I AM.
I'M DONE, TARA. I'VE HAD ENOUGH. I'VE DONE MY BIT FOR QUEEN AND COUNTRY.
YOU'LL KILL THE SECTION, IF YOU GO.
YOU CAN HANDLE IT.
ONE MINDER TO COVER THE WORLD? I'M GOOD, I'M NOT THAT GOOD.
MAYBE NOT THAT GOOD AT ALL. I DIDN'T DATE THE LETTER. I'LL WAIT UNTIL CROCKER'S FOUND A REPLACEMENT FOR BUTLER BEFORE TURNING IT IN.
YOU'LL HAVE TO STAY LONGER THAN THAT. I'LL NEED YOUR HELP TO BREAK IN THE NEW GUY.
YOU'LL BREAK HIM IN JUST FINE.
THE WAY I BROKE THE LAST ONE? OH, BRILLIANT THAT.

THAT WASN'T YOUR FAULT.

I GOT HIM *KILLED*, I'D THINK THAT'S *MY* FAULT. IF I'D *SEEN* THE BLOODY *TRUCK*--

YOU *DIDN'T* GET HIM KILLED.

I *DID*, I DAMN WELL *DID*, TOM--

NO. YOU *DIDN'T*.

SO THAT'S ENOUGH ABOUT THAT.

WHERE'S A DAMN *PEN*?

I *SWEAR* SOMEONE COMES IN HERE AND NICKS THEM.

HERE.

AH, THANKS.

WHAT DO YOU THINK? SHOULD I DO IT LIKE IN THE PRISONER?

YOU MEAN "DELIVERED BY HAND," AND ALL THAT?

EXACTLY.

WHEN I HIT THE *VILLAGE*, WHAT NUMBER YOU RECKON THEY'LL GIVE ME?

I'M HOPING FOR SOMETHING LIKE NUMBER *FOUR*, MAYBE.

I DON'T THINK THEY LET YOU *CHOOSE*, TOM.

BESIDES, YOU'RE *NOT* THAT DAMN *IMPORTANT*.

NUMBER FOUR HUNDRED AND EIGHTY-TWO, MORE LIKE.

DOESN'T HAVE QUITE THE *RING* AS NUMBER SIX, THOUGH, DOES IT?

NO. I'M AFRAID IT DOESN'T.

HEY, STOP THAT.

I'M NOT OUT OF HERE YET.

DREEET DREEET

ANSWER YOUR DAMN PHONE, MINDER ONE.

MINDER ONE.

YES, SIR, BOTH OF US.

WE'LL BE RIGHT UP.

BOTH MINDERS TO SEE YOU, SIR.

GOOD. NOW GO AWAY.

FEELING *BETTER*, ARE WE, TARA?

MUCH, SIR. TWENTY-FOUR HOUR *FLU*.

I HEARD IT'S *PARTICULARLY* SAVAGE IN BATH.

SIT, BOTH OF YOU.

MONDAY, FRANCES BARCLAY BECOMES OUR NEW C.

THAT'S THE...HE'S THE JIC CHAIR, ISN'T HE? THE ONE WHO WROTE THAT *REPORT* ON OPERATIONAL *FAILINGS*?

THAT'S HIM.

IT'S A *DONE* DEAL, BOSS?

IF MY MEAL WITH SIR WALTER SECCOMBE HADN'T CONVINCED ME, THE...DISCUSSION I HAD WITH SIR FRANCES AN HOUR OR SO AGO MADE IT *PERFECTLY* CLEAR.

THE *FIRST* THING OUR *NEW* C INTENDS TO DO IS *TIE* OUR *HANDS* BEHIND OUR BACKS, THEN *CHOP* THEM *OFF*.

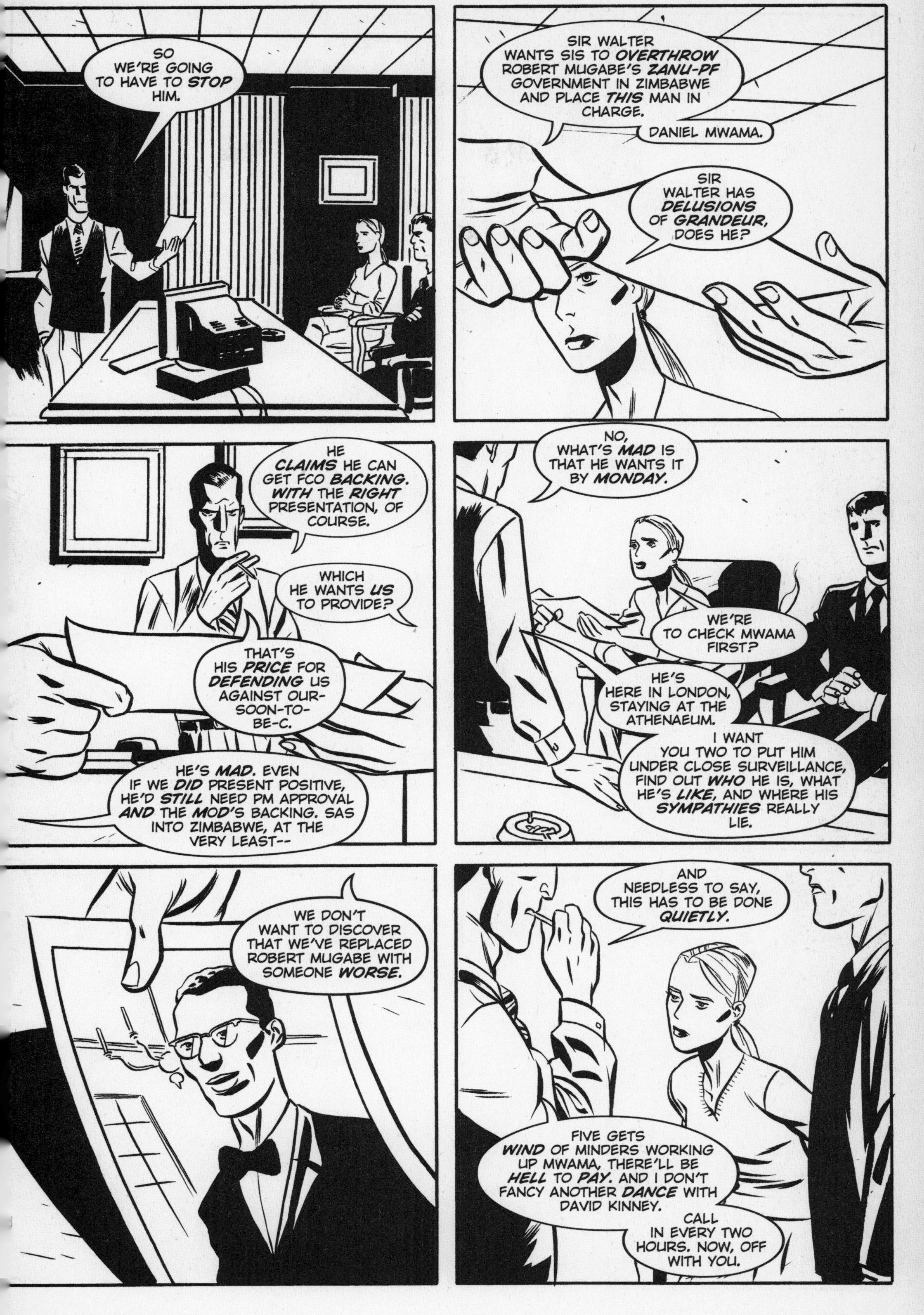

SO WE'RE GOING TO HAVE TO STOP HIM.
SIR WALTER WANTS SIS TO OVERTHROW ROBERT MUGABE'S ZANU-PF GOVERNMENT IN ZIMBABWE AND PLACE THIS MAN IN CHARGE.
DANIEL MWAMA.
SIR WALTER HAS DELUSIONS OF GRANDEUR, DOES HE?
HE CLAIMS HE CAN GET FCO BACKING. WITH THE RIGHT PRESENTATION, OF COURSE.
WHICH HE WANTS US TO PROVIDE?
THAT'S HIS PRICE FOR DEFENDING US AGAINST OUR-SOON-TO-BE-C.
HE'S MAD. EVEN IF WE DID PRESENT POSITIVE, HE'D STILL NEED PM APPROVAL AND THE MOD'S BACKING. SAS INTO ZIMBABWE, AT THE VERY LEAST--
NO, WHAT'S MAD IS THAT HE WANTS IT BY MONDAY.
WE'RE TO CHECK MWAMA FIRST?
HE'S HERE IN LONDON, STAYING AT THE ATHENAEUM.
I WANT YOU TWO TO PUT HIM UNDER CLOSE SURVEILLANCE, FIND OUT WHO HE IS, WHAT HE'S LIKE, AND WHERE HIS SYMPATHIES REALLY LIE.
WE DON'T WANT TO DISCOVER THAT WE'VE REPLACED ROBERT MUGABE WITH SOMEONE WORSE.
AND NEEDLESS TO SAY, THIS HAS TO BE DONE QUIETLY.
FIVE GETS WIND OF MINDERS WORKING UP MWAMA, THERE'LL BE HELL TO PAY. AND I DON'T FANCY ANOTHER DANCE WITH DAVID KINNEY.
CALL IN EVERY TWO HOURS. NOW, OFF WITH YOU.

I'LL MEET YOU IN THE PIT, TARA.

RIGHT.

IF THIS IS GOING TO BE A *LECTURE*, TOM, YOU CAN *SAVE* IT, ALL RIGHT?

WHAT, YOU MEAN ABOUT HOW SECCOMBE'S USING SIS TO FORWARD HIS OWN *POLITICAL* AGENDA?

OR ABOUT HOW THE HOME OFFICE WILL POSITIVELY *DETONATE* IF THEY HEAR YOU'VE GOT MINDERS WORKING UP A FOREIGN NATIONAL VISITING LONDON?

YES.

NAH, IT'S *NOT* ABOUT THAT.

I HAD AN INTERESTING CONVERSATION WITH JIM CHESTER YESTERDAY AFTERNOON.

PHONED YOU, DID HE?

OF COURSE HE BLOODY WELL PHONED ME! YOU'RE MY HEAD OF SECTION, YOU THINK HE WASN'T GOING TO GET MY PERMISSION FIRST?

THE ANSWER IS *NO*.

NO? NO *WHAT*, NO?

NO, YOU *CAN'T* LEAVE.

NO, I *DON'T* ACCEPT YOUR *RESIGNATION*.

I DON'T *CARE* IF YOU'VE BOUGHT A *BAR* OR A *BOAT* OR A BLOODY *HOUSE* IN THE COTSWOLDS, YOU'RE MY MINDER ONE, YOU'RE HEAD OF THE SPECIAL SECTION, AND YOU'RE *STAYING*.

NOW GET CHACE, FIND MWAMA, AND DIG UP *SOMETHING* ON HIM THAT I CAN *USE*.

I'LL STICK AROUND UNTIL YOU'VE FOUND A *REPLACEMENT* FOR BUTLER.

BUT, WITH ALL DUE RESPECT, SIR...

...I HAVE GIVEN MY *NOTICE*, AND IF YOU DON'T *LIKE* IT...

...YOU CAN GET *STUFFED*.

RAF CREDENHILL, HEREFORD, WALES.

...MOVEMENT, WE HAVE MOVEMENT *TWO* X-RAYS ON INDIGO THREE--

--*SHOTS* FIRED! SHOTS *FIRED!* YANKEE *DOWN,* ENTRY *GO GO GO*--

BREACH BREACH BREACH!

KRAAAK

X-RAY DOWN!

KRAK KRAK

KRAK KRAK KRAK KRAK

TWO X-RAY DOWN.

INDIGO TWO *CLEAR!*

X-RAY *DOWN* INDIGO ONE *CLEAR!*

ENTRY INDIGO *TWO,* C'MON, C'MON HART *MOVE* IT--

X-RAYS MOVING INDIGO *THREE,* TWO YANKEES, REPEAT *TWO* YANKEES--

FUCK *OFF,* POOLE.

INDIGO *TWO,* BREACH BREACH BREACH!

GO.

BREACH BREACH--

¡KRAK KRAK KRAK KRAK

--BREACH!

KRAK KRAK

INDIGO T... CLEAR, THRE... DOWN, TWO SECUR...

HNGG

SON OF A <HNNN> BITCH

POOLE! POOLE, ARE YOU ALL RIGHT?

CLEAR THE FLOOR, EVERYONE OFF THE FUCKING FLOOR!

POOLE? C'MON, MATE, YOU ALL RIGHT?

HOMO.

KRAK

WHAT THE *HELL*--

BLUE TWO, *HOLD* YOUR *FIRE!*

FRIENDLY HIT, FRIENDLY HIT!

MAKE *SAFE*, MAKE *SAFE!*

YOUR ARMOR *HELD,* C'MON, POOLE, *SHAKE* IT OFF.

I'M <KAFF> ALL RIGHT.

--EXPLAIN WHAT THE *HELL* HAPPENED IN THERE, HART?

SIR! ACCIDENTAL *DISCHARGE* OF MY *WEAPON*, SIR! AS I WAS ATTEMPTING--

ACCIDENT? IS THAT WHAT YOU *CALL* IT?

YOU'RE *FUCKING SAS*, YOU'RE *NOT* PERMITTED *ACCIDENTS!* YOU *STOPPED* WITH THE FUCKING *ACCIDENTS* WHEN YOU STOPPED WEARING *NAPPIES*, YOU--

HART!

BASTARD DID THAT ON *PURPOSE*--

GET *OFF* ME YOU *FUCKING ARSE* HOUND--

--*SLOT* YOU SWEAR TO GOD YOU'LL--

THAT'S *ENOUGH!*

THAT'S *ENOUGH*, RIGHT *NOW!*

HART, YOU'RE ON *TAPE*, LAD, THE *WHOLE* THING! AND IF IT IS DETERMINED YOU *DELIBERATELY* FIRED THAT *ROUND*, YOU'RE NOT FOR RTU, YOU'RE UP ON FUCKING *CHARGES*, BOY.

GET OUT, GET CHANGED, AND GET TO THE COMMANDER'S *OFFICE*.

WHAT'S *THAT* ALL ABOUT, THEN?

YOU KNOW HART, MATE...

...THINKS POOLE'S GONNA *STICK* IT TO HIM....

GYM

YOU'RE A *VERY* CLEVER GIRL, TARA CHACE...

...HE'S ON HIS WAY DOWN.

HNNN

MAY I *HELP?*

OH...

...PLEASE DO.

CHAPTER 3

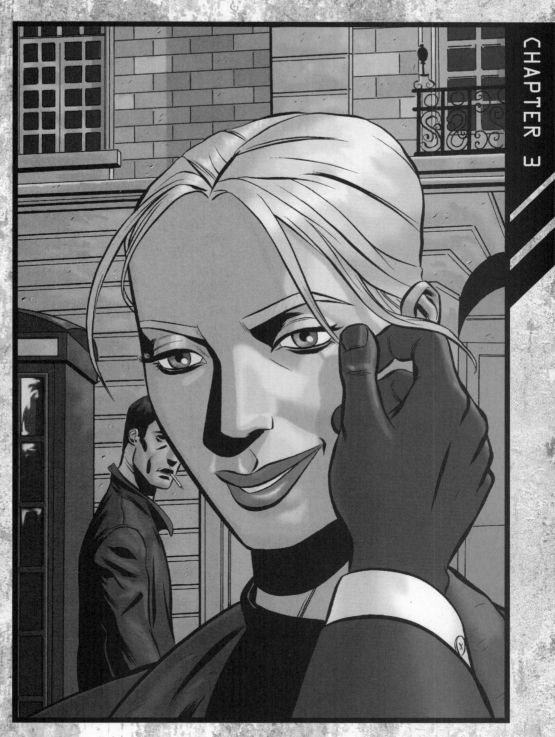

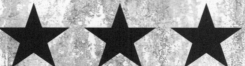

ANOTHER, SIR?

WHY NOT? MAKE IT THE ABERLOUR THIS TIME.

DON'T TAKE IT *SO* HARD, MATE. I'VE BEEN *STOOD-UP* MANY A TIME.

AT LEAST WE HAVE EACH *OTHER*, RIGHT?

FOR ANOTHER *HOUR* OR SO, YES, SIR.

IN THAT CASE, MAKE IT A *DOUBLE*.

...THINK I WOULD HAVE ENJOYED IT *MORE* IF I *UNDERSTOOD* THE *SOURCE* MATERIAL.

AH, BUT, DAVID, THAT'S WHAT I'VE BEEN *TRYING* TO EXPLAIN. IT'S SATIRIZING A *TALK-SHOW* FROM THE *STATES*, YOU SEE?

YES, I UNDERSTAND. BUT TELL ME *HONESTLY*, TRACY...

...THIS TALK-SHOW *NEVER* HAD JESUS CHRIST AS A GUEST, DID IT?

NOT TO MY KNOWLEDGE, DAVID, NO.

I AM *RELIEVED*. IT SEEMS SOMEHOW *UNBECOMING* OF THE SON OF GOD.

THANK YOU FOR YOUR *WONDERFUL* COMPANY THIS EVENING.

YOU SPARED ME THE *INDIGNITY* OF SEEING THE SHOW BESIDE AN *EMPTY SEAT.*

I'M *CERTAIN* YOU'D HAVE FOUND *SOMEONE* TO *FILL* IT.

PROBABLY, BUT I AM *FORTUNATE* THAT IT WAS *YOU.*

YOUR *BUSINESS* TOMORROW, DOES IT *EXTEND* INTO EVENING?

MY MEETINGS ARE FINISHED BY *THREE.*

I WOULD LIKE TO TAKE YOU TO *DINNER*, IF YOU WOULD *PERMIT* IT.

SAY, SEVEN O'CLOCK?

DAVID! DON'T YOU HAVE MEETINGS OF YOUR *OWN?*

I'M *SORRY*, I ONLY MEANT--

CALL ME AT *HALF* PAST THREE...

...ASK ME *AGAIN* THEN.

KEON, FIND OUT WHAT *ROOM* MISS CARLISLE IS STAYING IN...

...HAVE *TWO DOZEN* ROSES SENT TO HER IN THE MORNING, PLEASE. RED AND WHITE.

ABSOLUTELY, MISTER MWAMA.

YOU'VE **GOT TO BE KIDDING** ME.

THIS IS OVER **FIFTY QUID** IN **SCOTCH!**

WHAT CAN I SAY, BOSS? IT'S AN **EXPENSIVE** HOTEL.

NEXT TIME DRINK **WATER.**

YOU **BEEN** IN THE **ATHENAEUM?** I ASKED FOR **WATER,** I'D HAVE BEEN OUT ON MY **EAR.**

ANYWAY, WOULDN'T HAVE **WORKED.** HAD TO GIVE THE BARMAN A **SOB** STORY ABOUT HOW MY **DATE** HAD LEFT ME HIGH AND DRY.

DROWNING MY **SORROW** IN **WATER** WOULDN'T HAVE **WASHED,** PARDON THE **PUN.**

I SHUDDER TO THINK WHAT MINDER TWO'S **EXPENSE** REPORT WILL LOOK LIKE.

WELL, SHE **WON'T** BE BILLING **FOOD,** I'LL TELL YOU **THAT** MUCH...

BDEET

...MISTER DAVID MWAMA IS PLANNING ON **WINING** AND **DINING** HER AGAIN TONIGHT.

WHAT?

MINDER TWO, SIR.

ABOUT BLOODY TIME.

SORRY I'M *LATE* SIR.

OVERINDULGED LAST NIGHT, DID YOU?

NO, MORE LIKELY SHE HAD TO *MACHETE* HER WAY OUT OF HER *ROOM*. MWAMA SENT HER *TWO DOZEN* ROSES THIS MORNING.

HE DID, YES, BUT THAT'S NOT *WHY*.

I WAS *FOLLOWED* FROM THE HOTEL.

ONE OF THE *BODYGUARDS*?

DON'T THINK SO.

THEN WHO?

BOX.

BLOODY DAVID KINNEY.

R.A.F. CREDENHILL, HEREFORD.

SERGEANT POOLE. STEP INSIDE, PLEASE.

YES, SIR.

SO IT SEEMS WE HAVE A *PROBLEM*, SERGEANT POOLE.

ONE WHICH I HAVE TAKEN *STEPS* TO ADDRESS...

...AS YOU CAN *SEE*.

THAT'S *HART'S*.

HE'S BEEN *RETURNED TO UNIT*, AND WILL BE DISCIPLINED FURTHER *THERE*.

VERY GOOD, SIR.

DO YOU *THINK* SO?

HE'S BEEN *STRIPPED* OF HIS *BADGE* AND R.T.U.'D. DOES IT *END* THERE?

SIR?

I'VE *READ* THE ACCOUNTS OF WHAT HAPPENED IN THE KILLING HOUSE YESTERDAY, AND *REVIEWED* THE TAPES.

FROM THE *VIDEO* ALONE, IT IS *POSSIBLE* TO BELIEVE THAT CORPORAL HART *DISCHARGED* HIS WEAPON ON ACCIDENT. THAT HE *SHOT* YOU ON *ACCIDENT*.

IT IS *POSSIBLE* TO BELIEVE THAT...

...*UNTIL* ONE REVIEWS THE *AUDIO*.

DO YOU KNOW WHAT HE *SAID* PRIOR TO FIRING HIS WEAPON, SERGEANT?

NO, SIR, I DON'T.

HE SAID, "*HOMO*," SERGEANT POOLE.

BY WHICH IT SEEMS HE MEANT TO INDICATE THAT YOU ARE A *HOMOSEXUAL*.

I AM, SIR.

I KNOW.

DO YOU WISH TO PRESS *CHARGES* AGAINST CORPORAL HART, SERGEANT?

I AM CONSIDERING IT, SIR.

I SEE.

STAND AT EASE, POOLE, FOR GOD'S SAKE.

YOU'RE A *BRILLIANT* TROOPER, POOLE. I'M PLANNING ON MOVING YOU INTO THE *SABRE* SQUADRON AT THE NEXT *ROTATION*.

I CAN'T *DO* THAT IF YOU BRING *CHARGES* AGAINST CORPORAL HART.

WITH ALL DUE RESPECT, SIR, CORPORAL HART TRIED TO *KILL* ME.

AND *IF* HE TRIED TO KILL ME BECAUSE HE FEARS MY SEXUAL *ORIENTATION*, I FEEL I MUST PURSUE IT.

DON'T *OVERSTATE* IT, POOLE. IF HART HAD WANTED TO KILL YOU, HE'D HAVE PUT THE *BULLET* IN YOUR *NECK*, AND WE *BOTH* KNOW IT.

GOD KNOWS HE COULD HAVE *MADE* THE *SHOT*, THE SAME AS *YOU* OR I COULD.

HE DIDN'T WANT TO KILL YOU. HE WANTED TO *SHAME* YOU.

ALL THE MORE REASON FOR ME TO SPEAK OUT, SIR.

HART IS BEING *DEALT* WITH. ONCE HE'S *BACK* WITH HIS *UNIT*, HE'LL BE DEALT WITH *FURTHER*.

BUT IF YOU BRING *CHARGES* AGAINST HIM, YOU'LL BRING *PUBLICITY*, TOO, SERGEANT, IT'S A *GUARANTEE*. THE *M.O.D.* IS *STILL* TRYING TO *RECONCILE* THE *E.U.* RULING ON HOMOSEXUALITY, AND THE *MEDIA* HAS BEEN *WAITING* FOR A STORY JUST LIKE THIS.

AND A STORY LIKE THIS ABOUT THE *S.A.S.*? THE *GUARDIAN* WILL *WET* ITSELF IN EXCITEMENT.

WE'VE *ALREADY* HAD OUR SHARE OF *BAD PRESS*. NEMESIS AND MCNAB... CHRIST, POOLE! WE'VE HAD *MORE* THAN OUR SHARE!

I AM ASKING YOU *NOT* TO PURSUE THIS, NICK.

FOR THE *GOOD* OF THE REGIMENT, LET IT GO.

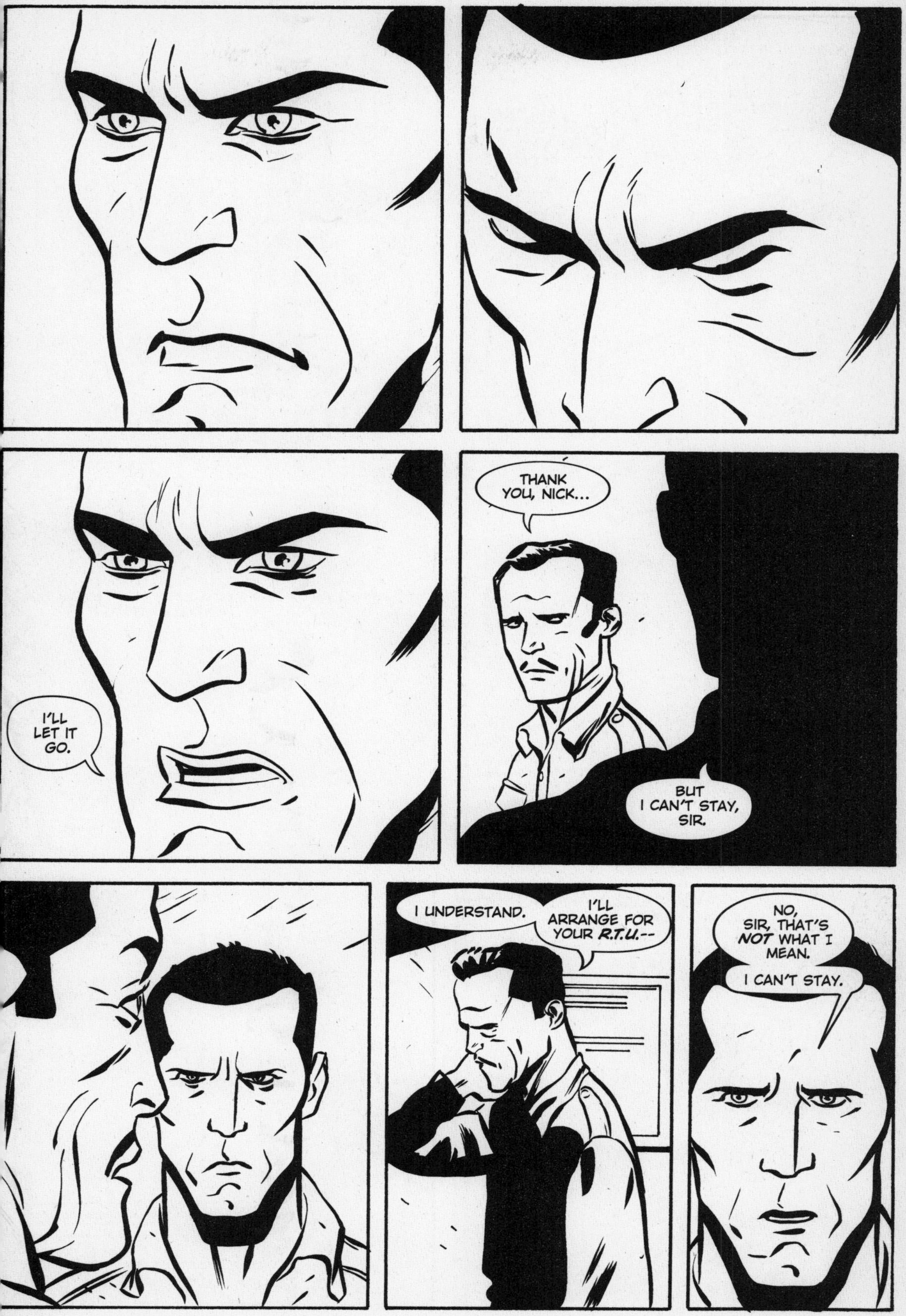
I'LL LET IT GO.
THANK YOU, NICK...
BUT I CAN'T STAY, SIR.
I UNDERSTAND.
I'LL ARRANGE FOR YOUR *R.T.U.*--
NO, SIR, THAT'S ***NOT*** WHAT I MEAN.
I CAN'T STAY.

COLONEL TRAVERS FOR COLONEL RICHARD MOSS, PLEASE...

JAMES, HOW ARE THINGS AT THE *S.P.T.?* PAUL CROCKER USING YOU TO *GOOD* EFFECT, I TRUST?

...WELL, BETTER *THAT* THAN *SIX MONTHS* IN THE *SAND*, I'D SAY...

...NO, NO, I QUITE AGREE....

LISTEN, RICHARD, I'VE HAD AN *INTERESTING* SITUATION ARISE HERE. I'VE A TROOPER I'M ABOUT TO *LOSE*, GOOD MAN, WITH SOMETHING IN THE NEIGHBORHOOD OF TEN *MILLION* OF HER MAJESTY'S POUNDS *INVESTED* IN HIM...

...I'D *HATE* TO SEE HIM GO TO *WASTE*....

PAUL, GOOD OF YOU TO COME OVER...

...I WAS *AFRAID* YOU'D BE TOO *BUSY.* PLEASE, HAVE A *SEAT.* WOULD YOU LIKE A *DRINK?*

NO, THANK YOU, SIR WALTER.

I EXPECT YOU KNOW WHY I WANTED TO SEE YOU?

YOU WANT TO KNOW WHERE WE ARE WITH DAVID MWAMA.

EXACTLY, AND I APPRECIATE YOUR *INDULGING* ME.

I DON'T HAVE *MUCH* TO REPORT AS YET.

THAT MAY BE BECAUSE THERE'S NOTHING TO FIND, PAUL.

TRUE, BUT THEN AGAIN, WE'VE HARDLY STARTED *LOOKING* AT HIM.

LOOKING AT HIM *HOW?*

I'VE PUT THE MINDERS ONTO HIS *SURVEILLANCE.* MINDER ONE IS BACKING UP MINDER TWO, WHO'S MANAGED TO GET *CLOSE* TO HIM.

I'M AFRAID I DON'T KNOW THEM.

MINDER ONE IS TOM WALLACE, HE HEADS THE SPECIAL SECTION. MINDER TWO IS TARA CHACE.

A *WOMAN.*

THAT'S THE *RUMOR.*

HOW CLOSE ARE WE TALKING ABOUT, PAUL?

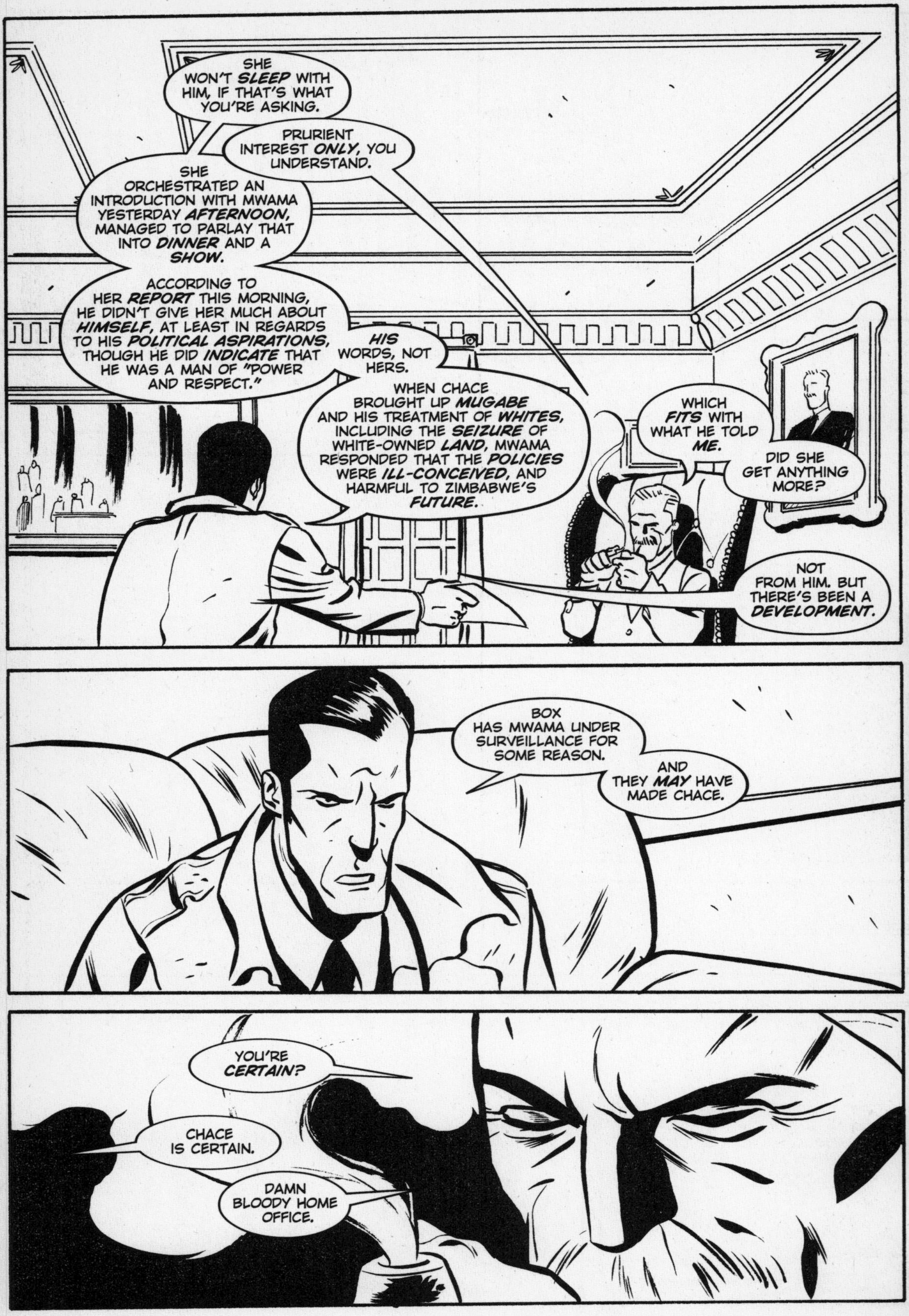
SHE WON'T SLEEP WITH HIM, IF THAT'S WHAT YOU'RE ASKING.
PRURIENT INTEREST ONLY, YOU UNDERSTAND.
SHE ORCHESTRATED AN INTRODUCTION WITH MWAMA YESTERDAY AFTERNOON, MANAGED TO PARLAY THAT INTO DINNER AND A SHOW.
ACCORDING TO HER REPORT THIS MORNING, HE DIDN'T GIVE HER MUCH ABOUT HIMSELF, AT LEAST IN REGARDS TO HIS POLITICAL ASPIRATIONS, THOUGH HE DID INDICATE THAT HE WAS A MAN OF "POWER AND RESPECT."
HIS WORDS, NOT HERS.
WHEN CHACE BROUGHT UP MUGABE AND HIS TREATMENT OF WHITES, INCLUDING THE SEIZURE OF WHITE-OWNED LAND, MWAMA RESPONDED THAT THE POLICIES WERE ILL-CONCEIVED, AND HARMFUL TO ZIMBABWE'S FUTURE.
WHICH FITS WITH WHAT HE TOLD ME.
DID SHE GET ANYTHING MORE?
NOT FROM HIM. BUT THERE'S BEEN A DEVELOPMENT.
BOX HAS MWAMA UNDER SURVEILLANCE FOR SOME REASON.
AND THEY MAY HAVE MADE CHACE.
YOU'RE CERTAIN?
CHACE IS CERTAIN.
DAMN BLOODY HOME OFFICE.

DID YOU PUT THEM ONTO HIM SOMEHOW?

WHY ON EARTH WOULD I DO THAT?

IMPATIENCE.

PAUL, LET ME *EXPLAIN* SOMETHING TO YOU THAT, I HOPE, WILL GUIDE OUR RELATIONSHIP IN THE *FUTURE*.

I'VE BEEN WITH THE FOREIGN OFFICE OVER *FORTY YEARS*. I'VE SEEN GOVERNMENTS COME AND GO, RISE AND FALL. I'VE WITNESSED TRIUMPHS, TRAGEDIES, AND *DISASTERS*.

WHEN I *HATCH* A *PLOT*, I DO IT *PROPERLY*.

AND THAT MEANS I *DON'T* INVOLVE THE HOME OFFICE.

UNDERSTOOD, SIR.

YOU'LL NEED TO FIND OUT *WHY* BOX IS INTERESTED, OF COURSE.

I DON'T SUPPOSE YOU'LL JUST *ASK* THEM?

IT WOULD AMOUNT TO CONFESSING THAT I'VE GOT MINDERS WORKING IN LONDON.

INDEED.

WELL, WHATEVER YOU DO, PAUL, I SUGGEST YOU DO IT *QUICKLY*.

FRANCES BARCLAY TAKES HIS *OFFICE* ON MONDAY.

THAT GIVES YOU JUST UNDER *THREE* DAYS.

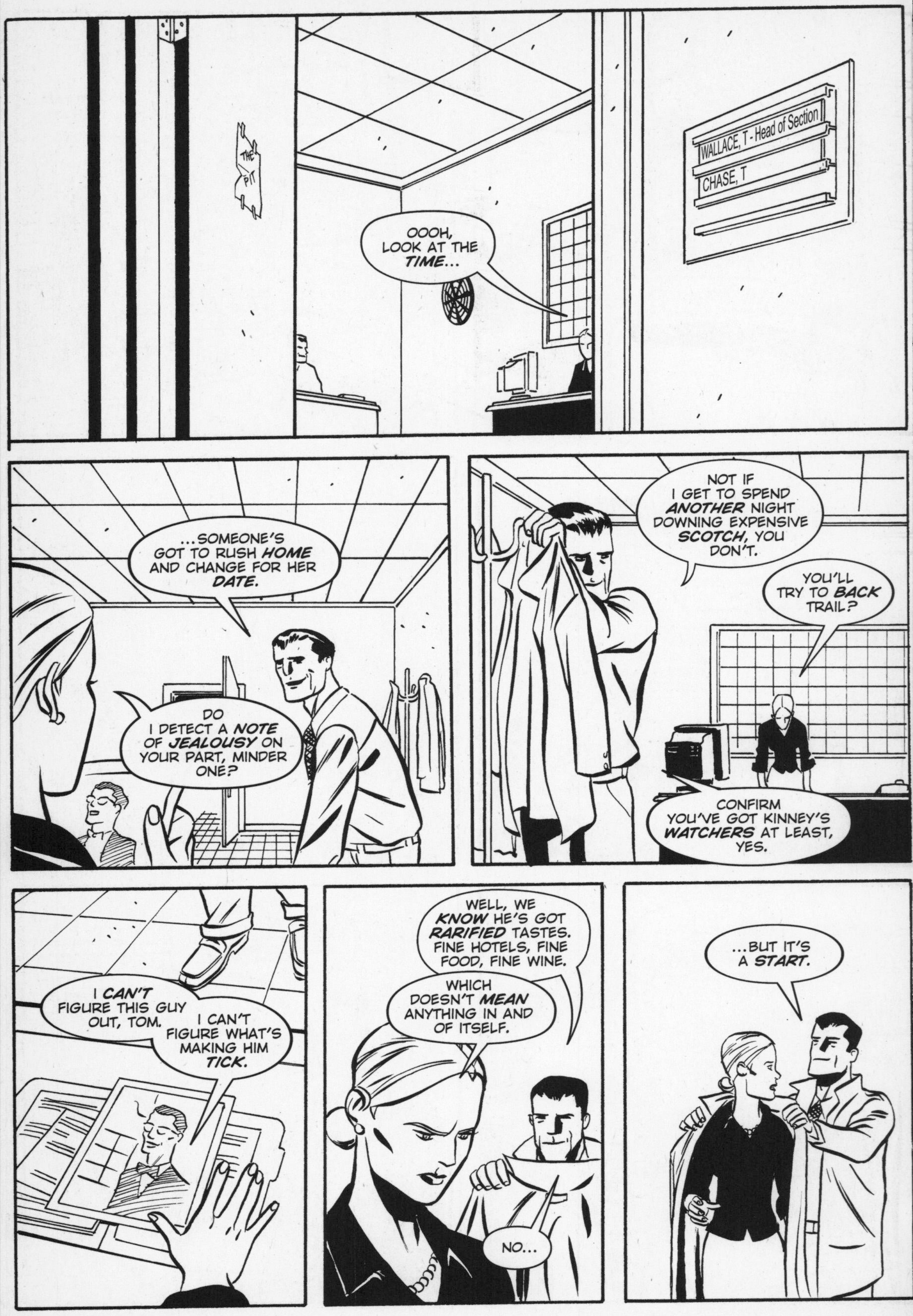
THE PIT
WALLACE, T - Head of Section
CHASE, T
OOOH, LOOK AT THE *TIME*...
...SOMEONE'S GOT TO RUSH *HOME* AND CHANGE FOR HER *DATE*.
DO I DETECT A *NOTE* OF *JEALOUSY* ON YOUR PART, MINDER ONE?
NOT IF I GET TO SPEND *ANOTHER* NIGHT DOWNING EXPENSIVE *SCOTCH*, YOU DON'T.
YOU'LL TRY TO *BACK* TRAIL?
CONFIRM YOU'VE GOT KINNEY'S *WATCHERS* AT LEAST, YES.
I *CAN'T* FIGURE THIS GUY OUT, TOM.
I CAN'T FIGURE WHAT'S MAKING HIM *TICK*.
WELL, WE *KNOW* HE'S GOT *RARIFIED* TASTES. FINE HOTELS, FINE FOOD, FINE WINE.
WHICH DOESN'T *MEAN* ANYTHING IN AND OF ITSELF.
NO...
...BUT IT'S A *START*.

NOK
NOK NOK NOK

JUST A MOMENT.

ATHENÆUM HO

OH, HELLO

I THOUGHT YOU WERE GOING TO *CALL* FIRST.

I'M *SORRY,* I CAN COME *BACK...*

NO, DON'T BOTHER. I WAS ABOUT TO GET *CHANGED,* IF YOU'D LIKE TO *WAIT.*

WE *ARE* STILL GOING FOR *DINNER,* ARE WE NOT?

IF YOU'RE STILL INTERESTED, YES, IT WOULD BE MY PLEASURE TO DINE WITH YOU.

OF COURSE I'M *STILL* INTERESTED, DAVID!

THANK YOU FOR THE *FLOWERS,* BY THE WAY...

...THEY'RE LOVELY.

WON'T BE A MOMENT.

FINE, FINE.

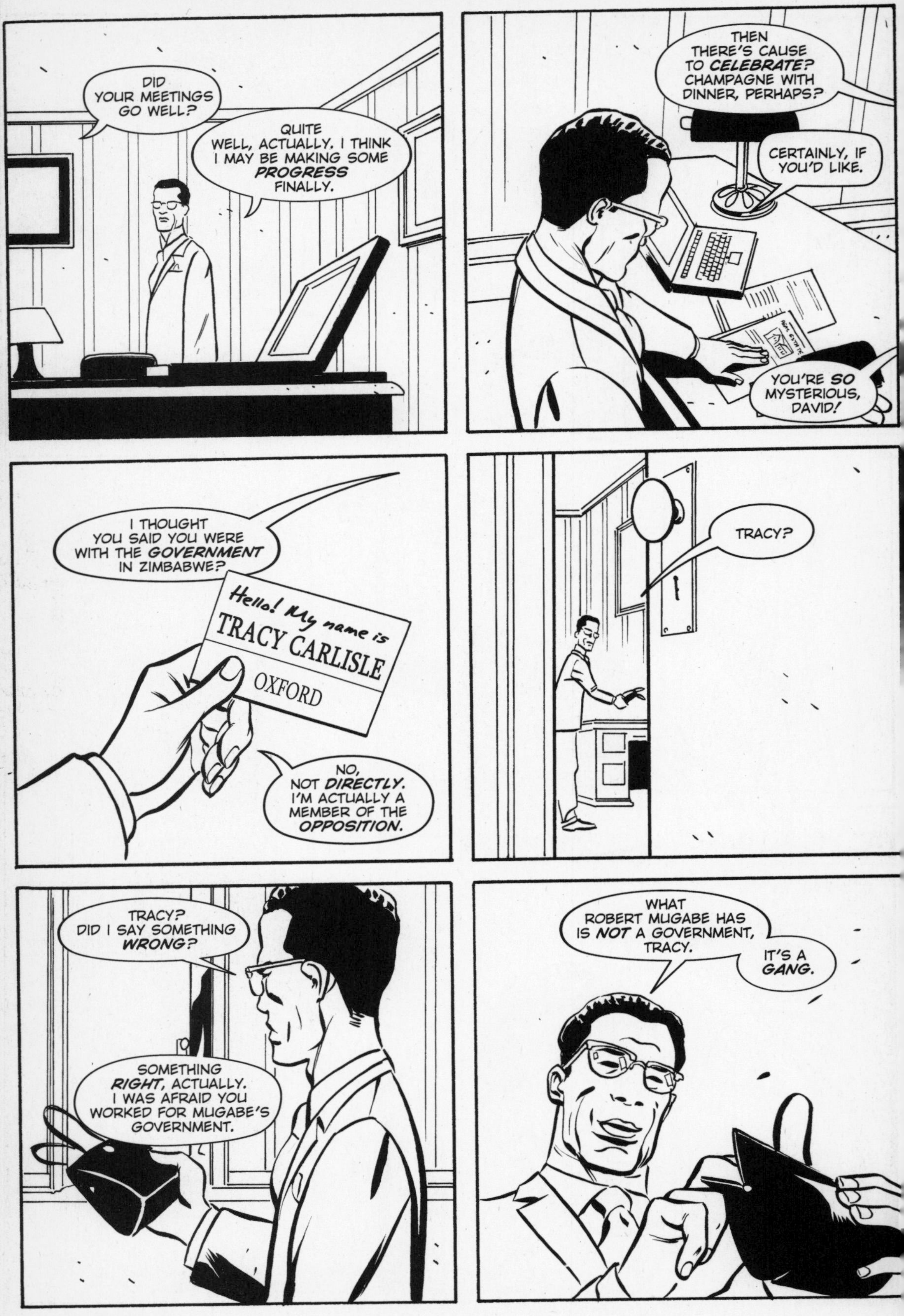
DID YOUR MEETINGS GO WELL?
QUITE WELL, ACTUALLY. I THINK I MAY BE MAKING SOME PROGRESS FINALLY.
THEN THERE'S CAUSE TO CELEBRATE? CHAMPAGNE WITH DINNER, PERHAPS?
CERTAINLY, IF YOU'D LIKE.
YOU'RE SO MYSTERIOUS, DAVID!
I THOUGHT YOU SAID YOU WERE WITH THE GOVERNMENT IN ZIMBABWE?
Hello! My name is
TRACY CARLISLE
OXFORD
NO, NOT DIRECTLY. I'M ACTUALLY A MEMBER OF THE OPPOSITION.
TRACY?
TRACY? DID I SAY SOMETHING WRONG?
SOMETHING RIGHT, ACTUALLY. I WAS AFRAID YOU WORKED FOR MUGABE'S GOVERNMENT.
WHAT ROBERT MUGABE HAS IS NOT A GOVERNMENT, TRACY.
IT'S A GANG.

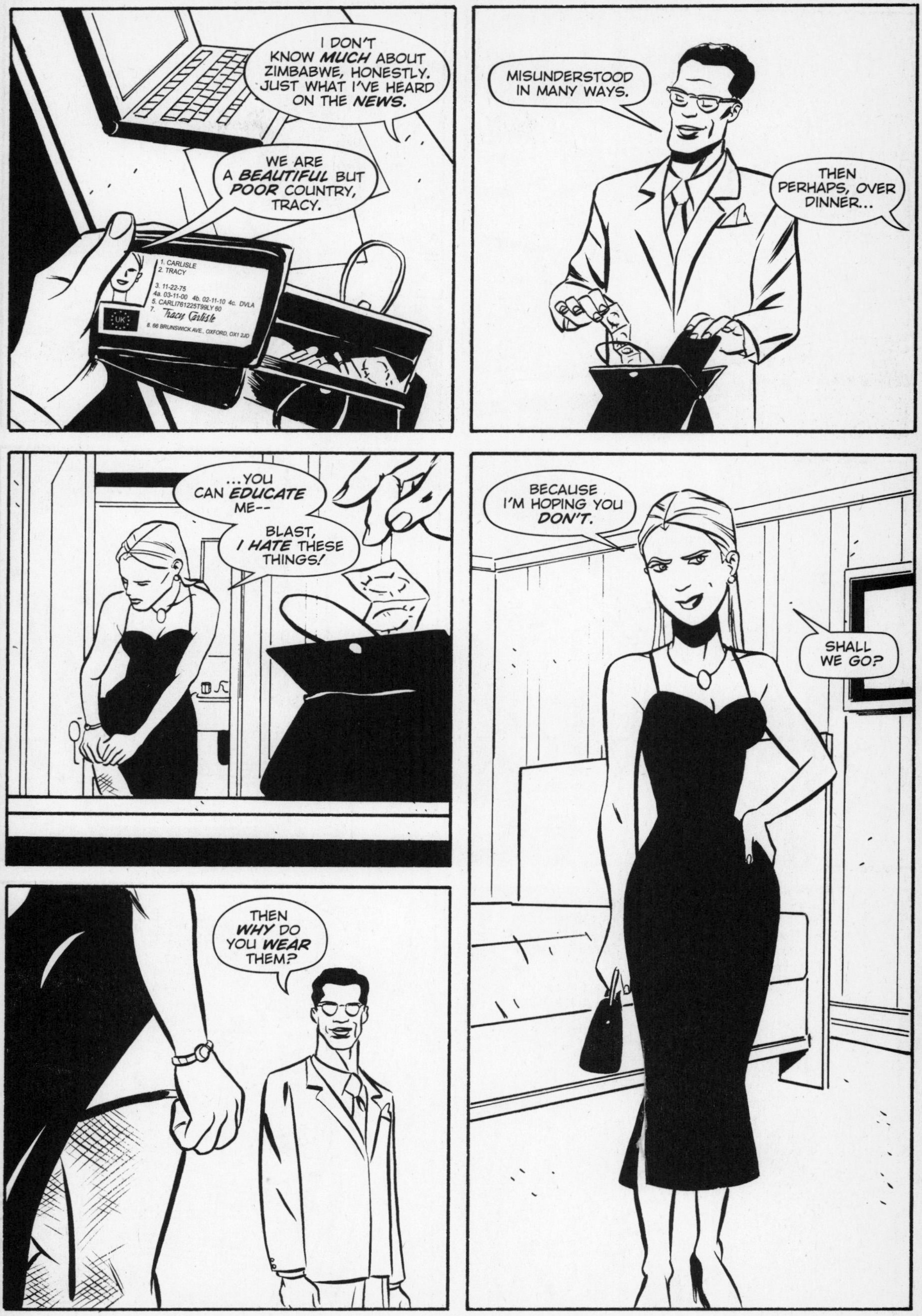
I DON'T KNOW MUCH ABOUT ZIMBABWE, HONESTLY. JUST WHAT I'VE HEARD ON THE NEWS.
WE ARE A BEAUTIFUL BUT POOR COUNTRY, TRACY.
1. CARLISLE
2. TRACY
3. 11-22-75
4a. 03-11-00 4b. 02-11-10 4c. DVLA
5. CARLI761225T99LY 60
7. Tracy Carlisle
UK
8. 66 BRUNSWICK AVE., OXFORD, OX1 2JD
MISUNDERSTOOD IN MANY WAYS.
THEN PERHAPS, OVER DINNER...
...YOU CAN EDUCATE ME--
BLAST, I HATE THESE THINGS!
THEN WHY DO YOU WEAR THEM?
BECAUSE I'M HOPING YOU DON'T.
SHALL WE GO?

WHAT?

COLONEL RICHARD MOSS TO SEE YOU, SIR.

SEND HIM THROUGH.

THANK YOU, KATE.

THESE NEED TO GO BACK TO MISSION PLANNING.

YES, SIR.

DICK, HAVE A SEAT.

GOOD TO SEE YOU, PAUL.

I'D SAY THE SAME IF I WASN'T SURPRISED TO SEE YOU IN THE FIRST PLACE.

WHY AREN'T YOU IN GOSPORT WITH THE S.P.T.?

THE SPECIAL PROJECTS TEAM IS FINE WITHOUT ME FOR A FEW HOURS.

I WAS ASKED TO PUT THIS IN FRONT OF YOU, AS A FAVOR.

FAVOR TO WHO?

RATHER NOT SAY, SIR.

THING IS, THE LAD IS LOOKING TO LEAVE THE ARMY. AND HIS C.O. THINKS, AND I AGREE, THAT IT WOULD BE A DAMN WASTE OF TALENT TO LET HIM GO.

WHAT'S WRONG WITH HIM?

HE'S GAY.

WE DON'T NORMALLY TAKE REFERRALS.

NO, I UNDERSTAND THAT, SIR.

I'LL TAKE IT UNDER ADVISEMENT, DICK, THAT'S ALL I CAN DO.

KATE WILL SHOW YOU OUT.

VERY GOOD, SIR. THANK YOU.

...BUT YOU MUST REMEMBER THAT MUGABE WAS *ELECTED* PRIME MINISTER IN *1980*, IN AN ELECTION THAT *YOUR* COUNTRY OVERSAW. IT WASN'T UNTIL '87 THAT HE *CHANGED* THE CONSTITUTION, RENAMING HIMSELF EXECUTIVE PRESIDENT.

IN OTHER WORDS, PRESIDENT FOR *LIFE?*

VERY MUCH SO, EXACTLY. THE *M.D.C.*, THE *MOVEMENT* FOR DEMOCRATIC *CHANGE*, FORMED IN *1999* AS AN *OPPOSITION* PARTY, BUT THEY--

--OR I SHOULD SAY, *WE*--HAVE BEEN *UNSUCCESSFUL* IN UNSEATING MUGABE, THOUGH HIS *GRIP* ON POWER IS *FINALLY* SLIPPING.

AND ONCE HE GOES, WHAT THEN?

AH, TRACY, *THAT* IS THE QUESTION OF THE HOUR. WHAT WILL MY COUNTRY BECOME AFTER MUGABE IS *GONE?* WHO WILL TAKE CONTROL?

SOMEONE IN THE *ZANU-PF*, I SHOULD THINK.

YES, YOU *WOULD* THINK THAT, BUT MUGABE'S BRAND OF SOCIALISM HAS *CRIPPLED* HIS OWN PARTY, YOU SEE? WHICH LEAVES THE *M.D.C.*..

BUT EVEN THERE, MORGAN TSVANGIRAI HAS MANY *RIVALS*....

DAVID... ...AM I HAVING *DINNER* WITH THE FUTURE PRESIDENT OF ZIMBABWE?

HA! *NO*, I WOULDN'T GO *THAT* FAR, TRACY...

...NOT *YET*, AT LEAST.

IN THAT CASE, I'LL *CHERISH* THIS MEAL.

SOMETHING TO TELL MY *GRANDCHILDREN* ABOUT WHEN I'M IN MY *DOTAGE*, THE NIGHT I ATE DINNER AT THE CONNAUGHT HOTEL WITH THE PRESIDENT OF ZIMBABWE...

...CERTAINLY I DOUBT I'LL *EVER* EAT *THIS* WELL AGAIN.

ONLY IF YOU *TIRE* OF MY *COMPANY*, TRACY...

...AS I *INTEND* TO EAT THIS WELL *EVERY* NIGHT.

SHALL I ORDER ANOTHER *BOTTLE* OF THE CHAMPAGNE?

BY ALL MEANS.

TOM WALLACE?

BEG PARDON?

MISTER WALLACE, THE *GENTLEMAN* WOULD LIKE TO HAVE A *WORD*, IF YOU *PLEASE*.

WHICH GENTLEMAN WOULD *THAT* BE, THEN?

MISTER KINNEY, SIR.

I BELIEVE YOU *KNOW* HIM.

HELL.

CHAPTER 4

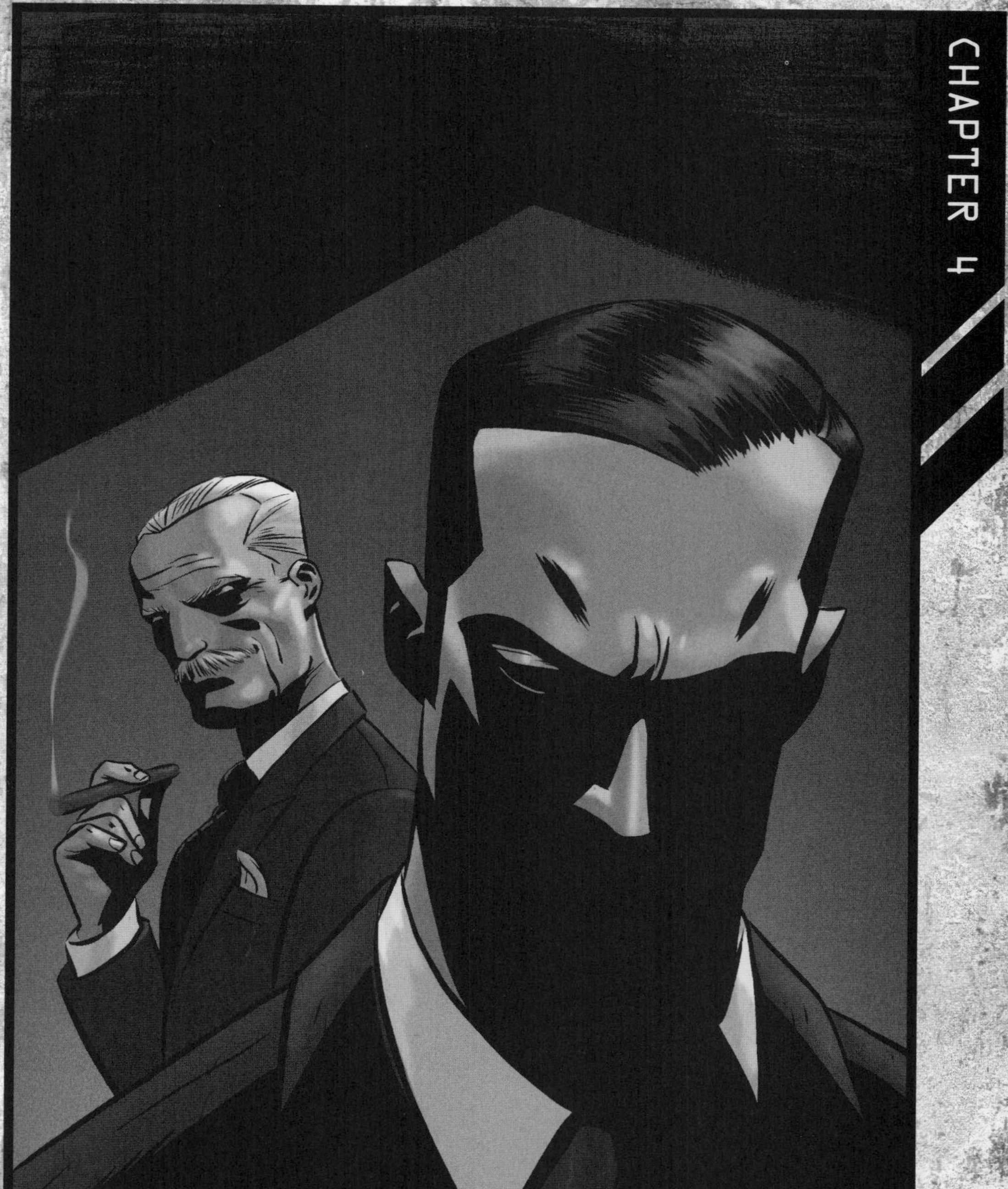

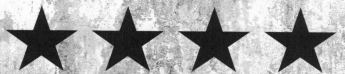

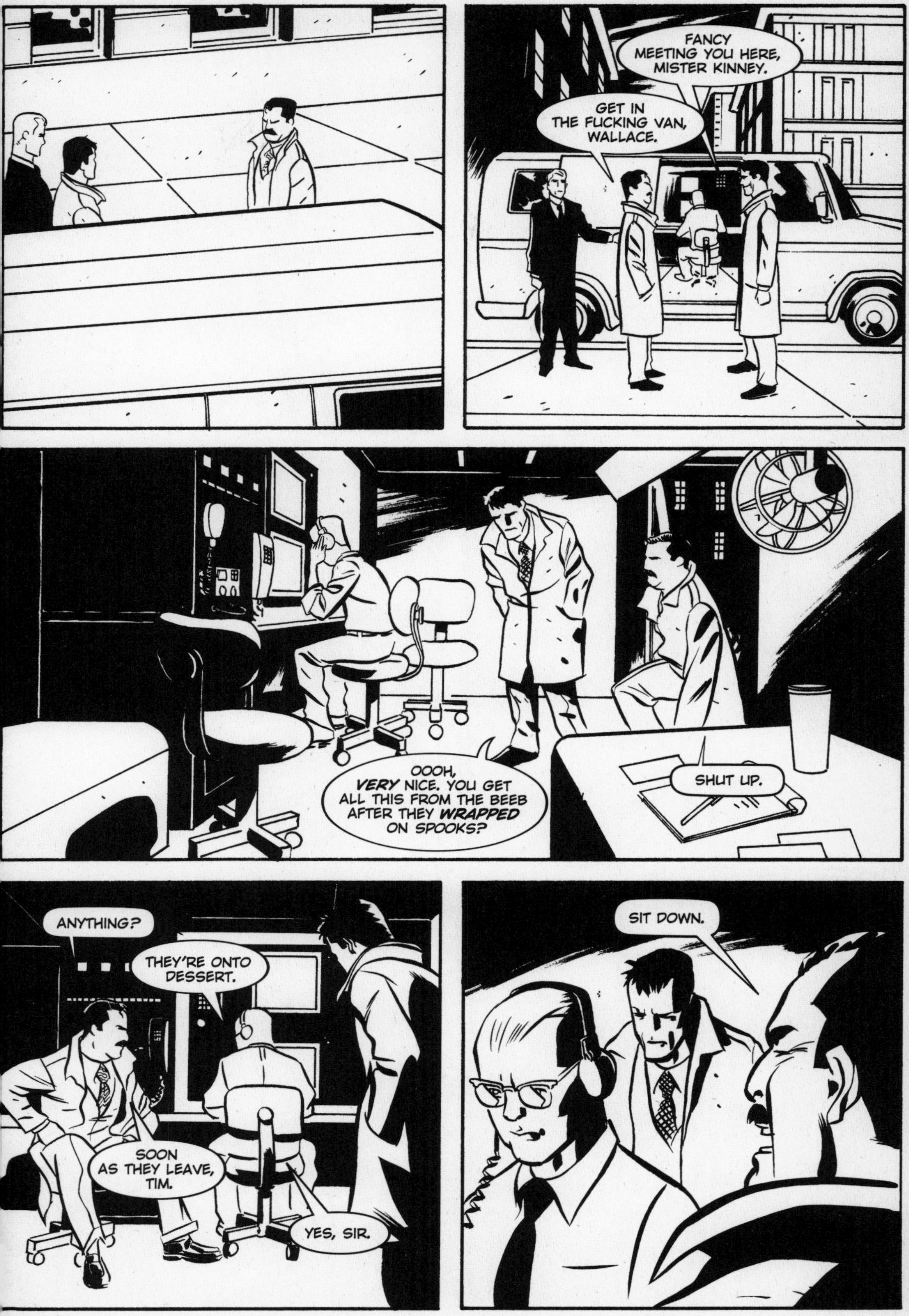
FANCY MEETING YOU HERE, MISTER KINNEY.
GET IN THE FUCKING VAN, WALLACE.
OOOH, VERY NICE. YOU GET ALL THIS FROM THE BEEB AFTER THEY WRAPPED ON SPOOKS?
SHUT UP.
ANYTHING?
THEY'RE ONTO DESSERT.
SOON AS THEY LEAVE, TIM.
YES, SIR.
SIT DOWN.

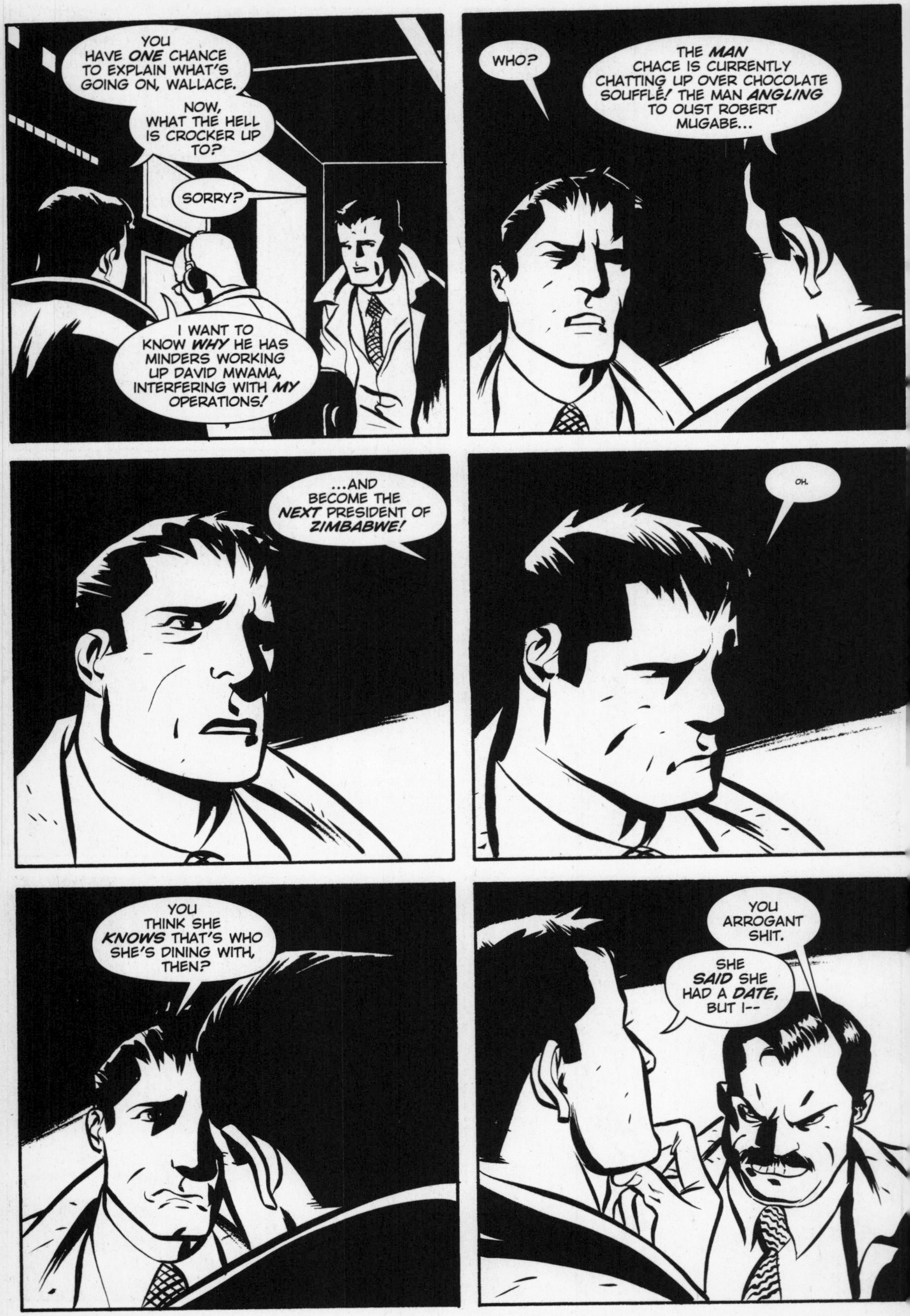
YOU HAVE ONE CHANCE TO EXPLAIN WHAT'S GOING ON, WALLACE.
NOW, WHAT THE HELL IS CROCKER UP TO?
SORRY?
I WANT TO KNOW WHY HE HAS MINDERS WORKING UP DAVID MWAMA, INTERFERING WITH MY OPERATIONS!
WHO?
THE MAN CHACE IS CURRENTLY CHATTING UP OVER CHOCOLATE SOUFFLÉ! THE MAN ANGLING TO OUST ROBERT MUGABE...
...AND BECOME THE NEXT PRESIDENT OF ZIMBABWE!
OH.
YOU THINK SHE KNOWS THAT'S WHO SHE'S DINING WITH, THEN?
YOU ARROGANT SHIT.
SHE SAID SHE HAD A DATE, BUT I--

GET OUT.

IT WAS *YOUR* CHOICE, AND YOU CHOSE *WRONG.*

YOU COULD HAVE COME *CLEAN,* BUT YOU WANTED TO BE *CUTE.*

MISTER KINNEY, I *DON'T KNOW* WHAT YOU'RE TALKING ABOUT--

DON'T *WORRY* YOURSELF, WALLACE. THE HOME SECRETARY *WILL.*

I'LL MAKE *CERTAIN* OF THAT.

I'LL MAKE *CERTAIN* HE KNOWS *EXACTLY* WHAT *SIS* HAS BEEN UP TO.

I'LL *STRESS* TO HIM *SIS'S HONESTY* AND *WILLINGNESS* TO COOPERATE.

NOW, GET *CHACE* OUT OF *THERE.*

OR ELSE I'LL HAVE HER *PICKED UP* FOR SOLICITING.

...INFLATION IS *OVER* FIVE *HUNDRED* PERCENT ANNUALLY.

OVER *HALF* OF ZIMBABWE'S CITIZENS REQUIRE *FOOD* AID, AND ALMOST SEVENTY-FIVE *PERCENT* ARE *UNEMPLOYED.*

THE SITUATION IS, SIMPLY, *INTOLERABLE.*

THEN *HOW* IS IT MUGABE HAS *REMAINED* IN POWER? WHY HAVEN'T THE *PEOPLE* REMOVED HIM?

IT'S *NOT* LIKE IT IS *HERE*, YOU HAVE TO UNDERSTAND.

MUGABE IS *BRUTAL*. HE *DESTROYS* HIS *OPPOSITION* THROUGH INTIMIDATION, TORTURE... EVEN *MURDER.*

I CAN'T... I JUST *CAN'T* IMAGINE IT.

MY GOD, DAVID...IF *YOU'RE* PART OF THE *OPPOSITION...*

...DOES THAT MEAN *YOUR* LIFE IS IN DANGER?

NOT AS *MUCH* AS SOME, *MORE* THAN OTHERS.

I HAVE BEEN *CAREFUL*, TRIED TO KEEP A *LOW* PROFILE, AS YOU WOULD SAY.

EAT, TRACY. IT'S *BETTER* WHEN IT'S *HOT.*

I'M *AFRAID* I'M NOT VERY *HUNGRY*.

IT WOULD BE A *CRIME* TO WASTE A *CHOCOLATE* SOUFFLÉ.

HOW CAN YOU *JOKE?* IT'S *YOUR* COUNTRY, *YOUR* LIFE.

I KEEP THINGS IN *PERSPECTIVE,* THAT'S HOW. I KNOW WHAT *MATTERS,* AND WHAT DOES *NOT.*

AND A CHOCOLATE SOUFFLE, *THAT* MATTERS?

YES, IN ITS *WAY.* WE *ALL* SEEK *COMFORT,* TRACY.

IN A *FINE* WINE OR A *RICH* DESSERT OR A *BEAUTIFUL* COMPANION...

...WE MUST MAKE THE *MOST* OF WHAT WE *HAVE.*

AND *IF* YOU HAVE *NOTHING?*

THERE IS *ALWAYS* SOMETHING. SOMETIMES YOU JUST HAVE TO *DIG* FOR IT....

'A *DEE DA DA* da *DEE da*

DAMN, SORRY...

...*BLOODY MOBILE*....

TRACY.

GET OUT NOW. MAKE WHATEVER *EXCUSE* YOU HAVE TO.

WHAT'S HAPPENED?

DAVID *BLOODY* KINNEY'S HAPPENED, AND IF YOU'RE NOT OUT OF THERE IN THE NEXT *FIVE* MINUTES, HE'LL HAVE YOU *DONE* FOR SOLICITING.

CALM DOWN. HAVE YOU CHECKED WITH THE *NEIGHBORS?*

GOOD GIRL.

NO, LOOK, I'LL GET THERE AS SOON AS I CAN.

HAS SOMETHING HAPPENED?

MY *MOTHER...*

Deet

...SHE'S *WANDERED* OFF. ALZHEIMER'S.

I'VE GOT TO GET BACK TO OXFORD, I'M SORRY. MY *SISTER* IS IN NEAR-HYSTERICS.

OF COURSE, I UNDERSTAND.

WILL YOU BE *RETURNING* TO THE HOTEL?

I DON'T *KNOW.* I'LL TRY TO LEAVE YOU A *MESSAGE.*

THANK YOU FOR DINNER, DAVID.

SORRY TO RUIN YOUR *SOUFFLÉ*.

ENOUGH ABOUT THE FUCKING *SOUFFLÉ*, I DON'T EVEN *LIKE* FUCKING CHOCOLATE FUCKING SOUFFLÉ.

WHAT HAPPENED?

KINNEY HAD ONE OF HIS *LADS* PUT THE *ARM* ON ME, WE HAD A *CHAT*.

THEY'RE WORKING UP SOMETHING ON MWAMA THEMSELVES...

...DIDN'T TAKE KINDLY TO US *MUDDYING* THEIR *WATERS*.

THEY'RE RUNNING AN *ACTUAL* OPERATION ON HIM?

THEY'VE PULLED OUT THE *STOPS*. THEY WERE EAVESDROPPING ON YOUR *DINNER*.

SO I HOPE YOU DIDN'T SAY ANYTHING YOU MIGHT REGRET.

I DIDN'T EVEN SEE THEM. CHRIST, *HOW* DID I *MISS* THAT?

COME IN ALREADY.

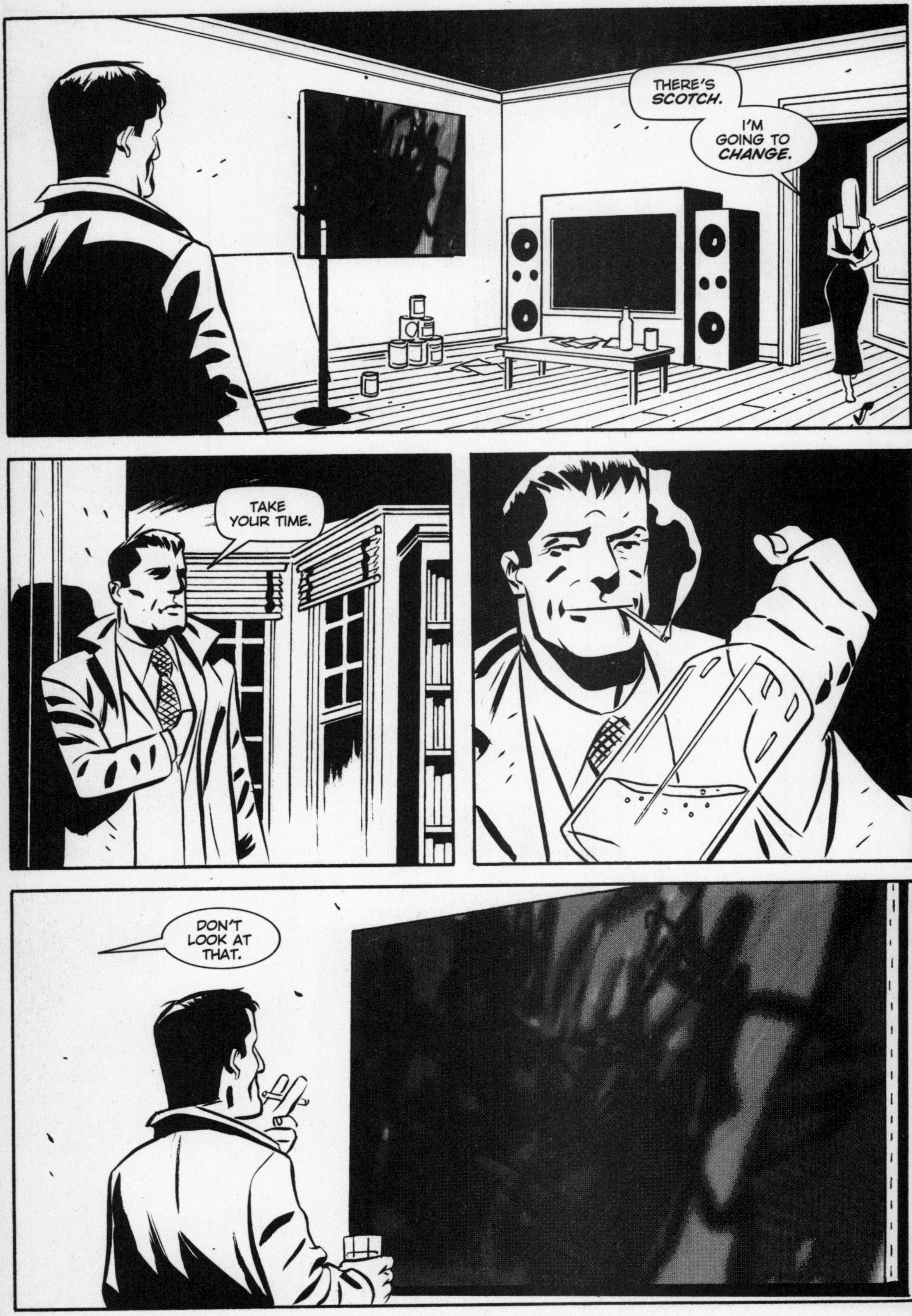
THERE'S SCOTCH.
I'M GOING TO CHANGE.
TAKE YOUR TIME.
DON'T LOOK AT THAT.

IT'S *SHIT.*

WHAT IS IT?

IT'S A *REFLECTION* ON THE *TRANSIENT* NATURE OF *LOVE* AND *VIRGINITY* AS COMMODITY IN THE *MODERN* WORLD.

REALLY?

NO, IT'S *SHIT.* LIKE I *SAID.*

SO WHAT NOW? WE CALL THE BOSS?

ALREADY DID.

AND?

AND HE *SWORE* A LOT, MUTTERED ABOUT HAVING A *WORK-AROUND,* AND THEN SAID HE'D SEE US AT *NINE* TOMORROW.

TOMORROW'S *SATURDAY.*

HE DIDN'T SEEM TO *CARE.*

SEE YOU IN THE MORNING, LOVE.

MAY I HELP YOU, SIR?

MY NAME'S *POOLE.* I'M... I'M *EXPECTED,* I THINK.

IDENTIFICATION, PLEASE, SIR.

RIGHT, OF COURSE.

VERY GOOD, MISTER POOLE.

THIS WILL GET YOU THROUGH THE DOORS, SIR.

PROCEED TO THE *CHECKPOINT*, WHERE YOU'LL *SURRENDER* YOUR *ENTRY* PASS AND RECEIVE A *VISITOR'S PERMIT*.

ONE OF THE *WARDENS* WILL ESCORT YOU THROUGH THE *BUILDING*.

PLEASE DO NOT *LEAVE* YOUR ESCORT, SIR, OR *DISOBEY* HIS *INSTRUCTIONS*, IS THAT *UNDERSTOOD*?

YES, PERFECTLY.

HAVE A *NICE* DAY, SIR.

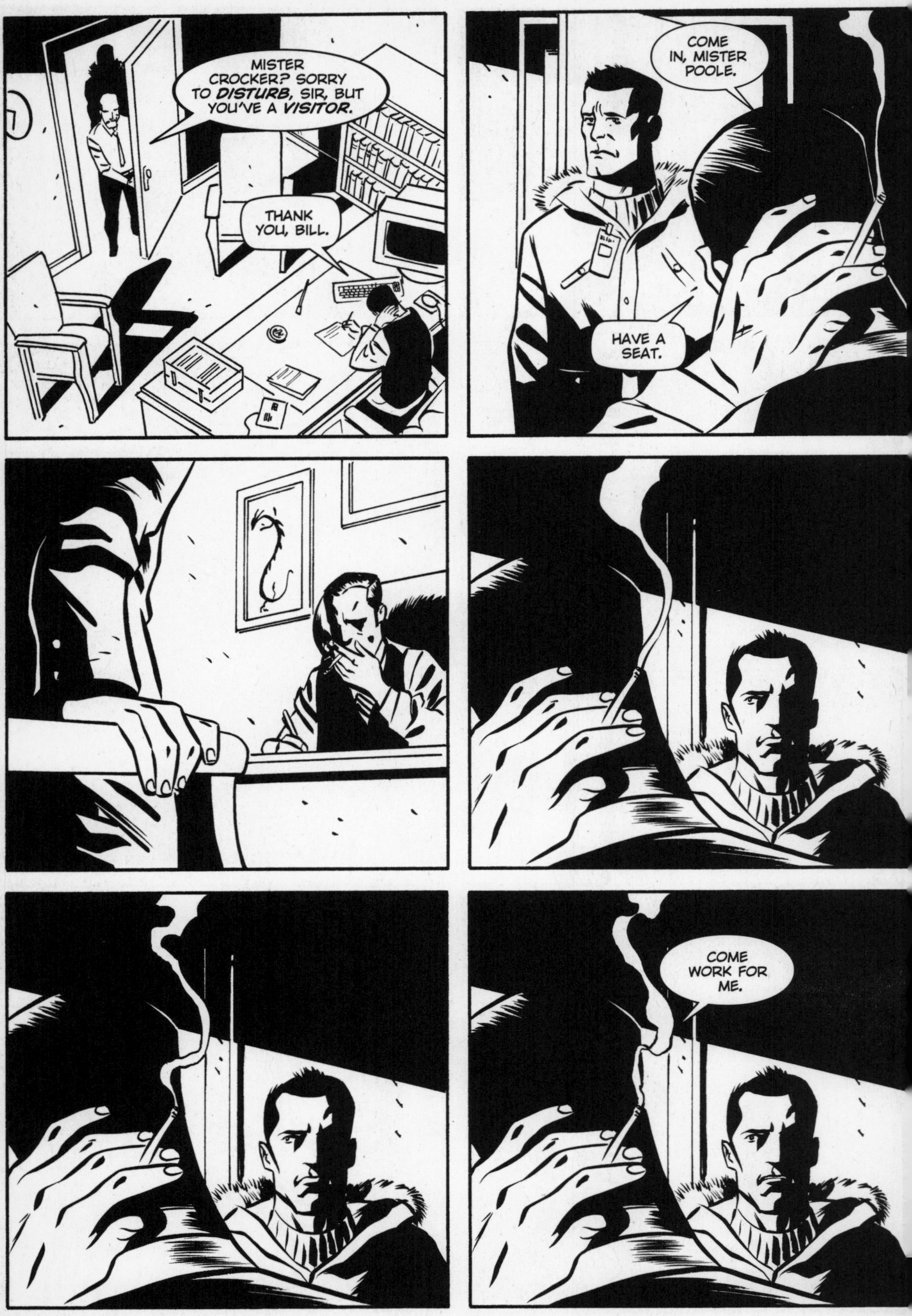
MISTER CROCKER? SORRY TO DISTURB, SIR, BUT YOU'VE A VISITOR.
THANK YOU, BILL.
COME IN, MISTER POOLE.
HAVE A SEAT.
COME WORK FOR ME.

I'M SORRY?

I WANT YOU TO WORK FOR ME.

AND *WHO* ARE YOU?

I MEAN, I *UNDERSTAND* YOU MUST BE OF *SOME* IMPORTANCE IN *SIS*, BUT YOU'LL HAVE TO FORGIVE ME, I REALLY HAVEN'T THE *FIRST* IDEA WHO YOU *ARE*.

I'M THE *DIRECTOR* OF *OPERATIONS*, MISTER POOLE.

ALL OPERATIONS. FROM THE *SLEEPER* IN BEIJING TO THE *STRINGER* IN CALCUTTA, THEY *ALL* BELONG TO *ME*.

MY NAME IS PAUL CROCKER.

NICK POOLE, PLEASURE TO MEET YOU, SIR.

IF IT *IS* NOW, IT WON'T BE FOR *LONG*.

AS D-OPS, I CONTROL NOT *ONLY* AGENTS IN THE *FIELD*, BUT A *SPECIAL SECTION* HERE AT HOME, *TASKED* DIRECTLY BY ME, *RESPONSIBLE* SOLELY TO *ME*, UTILIZED FOR *SPECIAL* OPERATIONS.

A SPECIAL OP IS A VERY *SPECIFIC* KIND OF *MISSION*, NICK.

INVARIABLY *HIGH-RISK*, HIGH-*STRESS*, WITH *NO* GUARANTEE OF *SUCCESS*. FAILURE CAN MEAN ANYTHING FROM *IMPRISONMENT* TO *DEATH* FOR THE OFFICER INVOLVED.

THEY'RE *RARE*, AS YOU MIGHT EXPECT.

BUT WHEN THEY HAPPEN, THEY HAVE TO BE DONE *RIGHT*.

THE OFFICERS WHO TAKE THESE MISSIONS ARE KNOWN IN-HOUSE AS *MINDERS*.

NORMALLY, THERE ARE *THREE* OF THEM.

'NORMALLY?'

WE'RE *SHORT* ONE AT THE MOMENT.

WHAT HAPPENED?

HE *DIED*.

SO DID THE ONE *BEFORE* HIM.

WHY ME? WHY NOT SOMEONE ALREADY *TRAINED* FOR *SIS*?

WE CAN *RETRAIN* YOU. YOU WERE *BADGED* WITH THE *SAS*, YOU'VE GOT *HALF* THE KNOWLEDGE YOU'D NEED *ALREADY*.

THAT DOESN'T ANSWER MY QUESTION, SIR.

NO, IT DOESN'T.

I NEED SOMEONE *NOW*, NICK, AND THERE'S NO ONE AT THE SCHOOL WHO'S *CLOSE* TO READY. FROM *EVERYTHING* I'VE READ IN YOUR *FILE*, YOU'D BE DAMN *GOOD* AT IT.

BUT MOSTLY BECAUSE YOU'D GO TO *WASTE* DOING *ANYTHING* ELSE.

MAY I HAVE SOME TIME TO THINK ABOUT IT?

I'M SORRY, NO.

IF I MAY, SIR, *HOW* DID I COME TO YOUR *ATTENTION?*

YOU *DID,* AND THAT'S *ALL* THAT SHOULD CONCERN YOU AT THE MOMENT.

I WON'T SING AND DANCE, NICK. I NEED AN *ANSWER,* AND I NEED AN ANSWER *NOW.*

COME WORK FOR ME.

OR WOULD YOU *RATHER* SELL *YOURSELF* TO *SANDLINE,* SPEND THE REST OF YOUR LIFE AS A *MERCENARY?*

OR MAYBE YOU FANCY GETTING INTO THE *PERSONAL PROTECTION* BUSINESS? GUARD A *ROYAL,* WRITE A *BOOK?*

I HADN'T QUITE *GOT* THAT FAR, SIR.

ALL RIGHT.

GOOD. WELCOME TO *SIS.*

THANK YOU, SIR.

YOU TWO CAN COME IN, NOW.

TARA CHACE, TOM WALLACE, MISTER POOLE.

MINDER TWO AND MINDER ONE, RESPECTIVELY.

TARA, TOM, THIS IS NICK POOLE.

MINDER THREE-- PROVISIONAL.

TOM'S FINE. AND YOU CAN CALL HER ANYTHING YOU LIKE.

BUT YOU'LL FIND I ONLY ANSWER TO TARA.

NICE TO MEET YOU, NICK.

YOU AS WELL.

RIGHT, THAT'S ENOUGH.

ALL OF YOU, SIT.

YOU'RE GETTING CHUCKED IN THE DEEP END, LAD.

SHUT UP, TOM.

RIGHT.

NICK, THERE'S SOMETHING I WANT YOU TO DO....

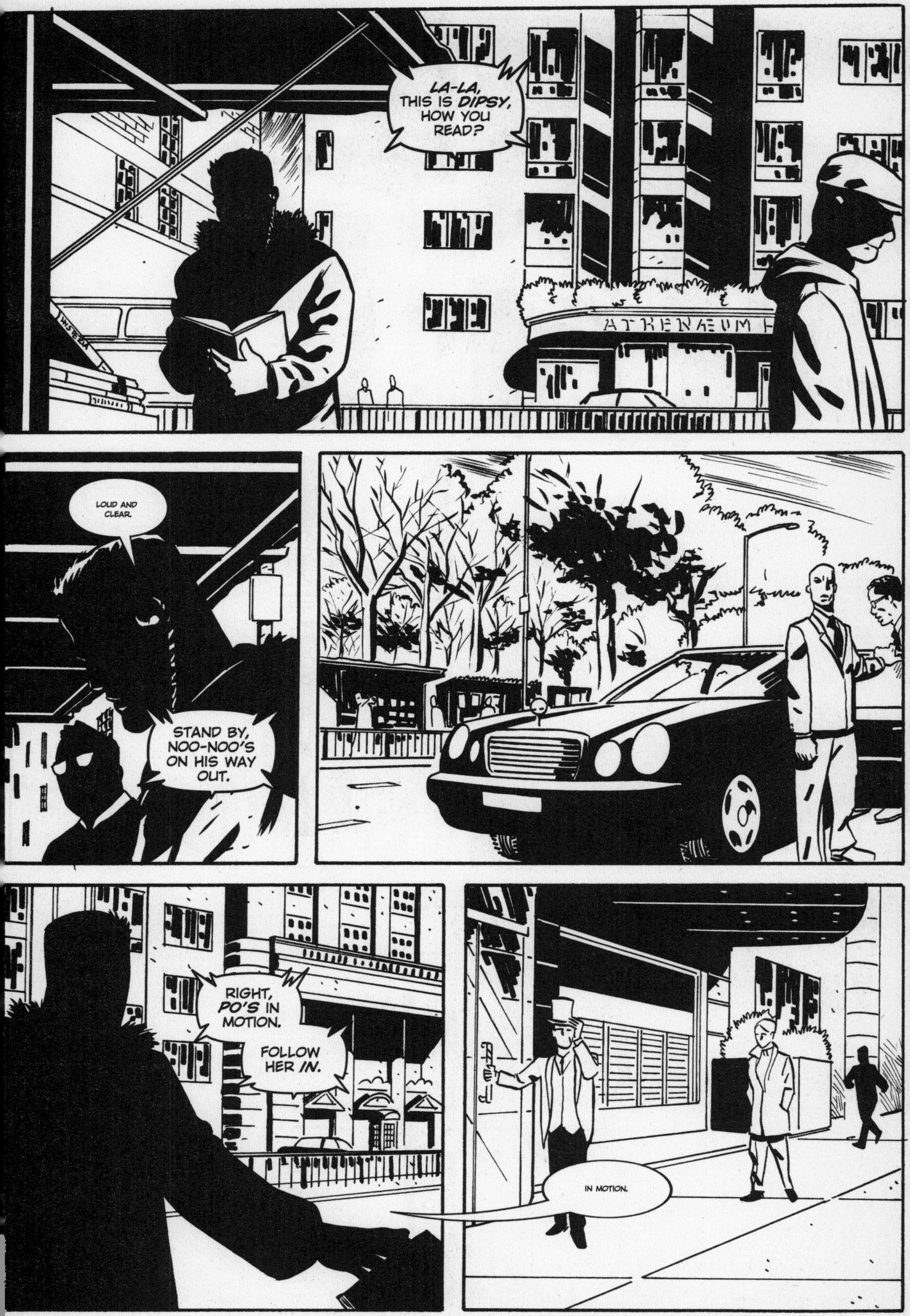
LA-LA, THIS IS DIPSY, HOW YOU READ?
LOUD AND CLEAR.
STAND BY, NOO-NOO'S ON HIS WAY OUT.
RIGHT, PO'S IN MOTION.
FOLLOW HER IN.
IN MOTION.

WELCOME BACK, MISS CARLISLE.

THANK YOU.

CARLISLE, ROOM 232--

HOLD ON.

I BEG YOUR PARDON?

YOU WERE WARNED OFF ONCE ALREADY.

WHAT'S IT TAKE FOR YOUR LOT TO GET THE HINT?

I CAME BACK TO BLOODY CHECK OUT! I'VE STILL GOT MY THINGS UP IN MY ROOM, YOU HALF-WIT THUG!

THEN YOU WON'T MIND IF I ACCOMPANY YOU, JUST TO MAKE SURE?

IS THERE A PROBLEM?

OF COURSE THERE'S A BLOODY PROBLEM, CAN'T YOU TELL THERE'S A PROBLEM...

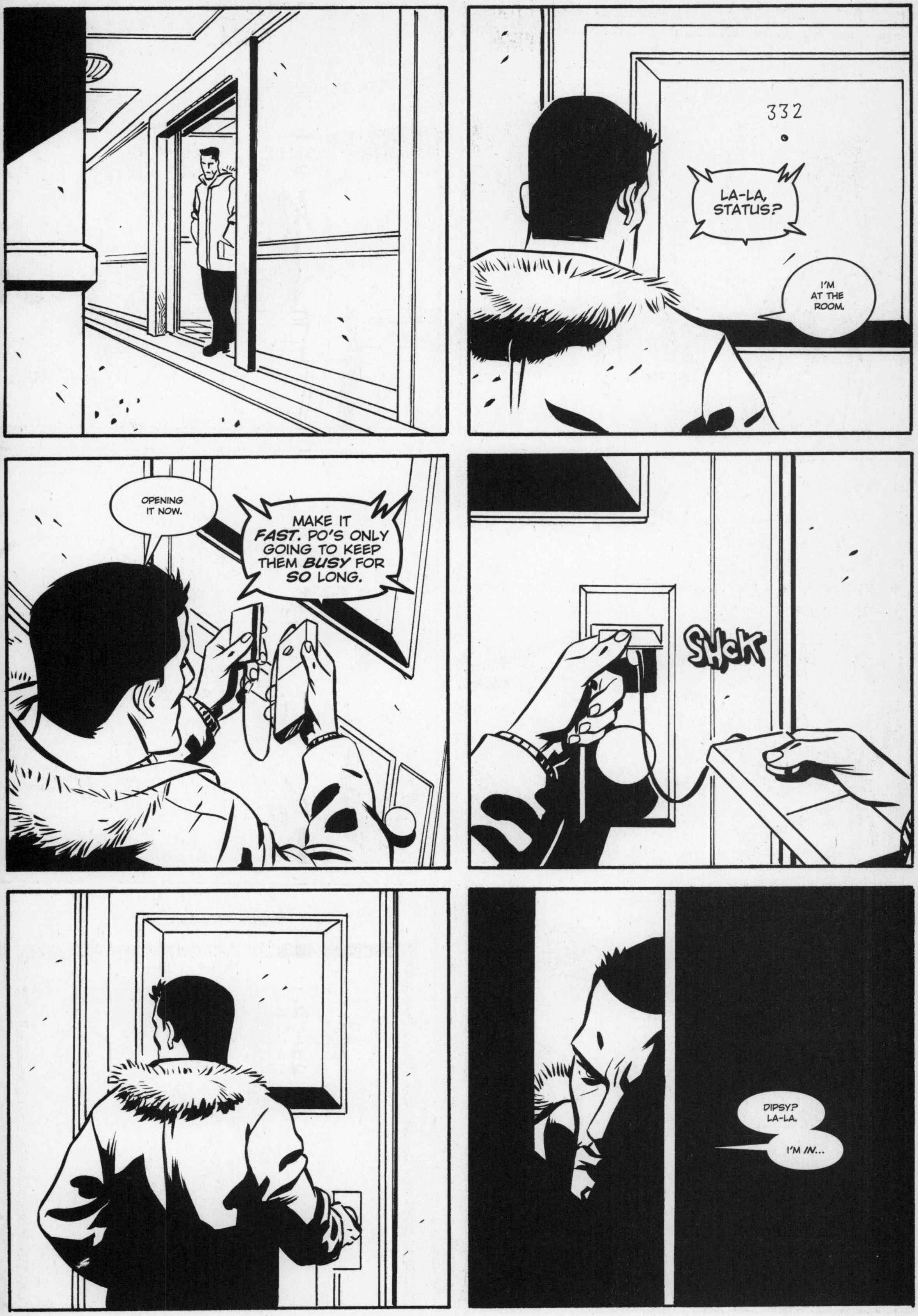
332
LA-LA, STATUS?
I'M AT THE ROOM.
OPENING IT NOW.
MAKE IT FAST. PO'S ONLY GOING TO KEEP THEM BUSY FOR SO LONG.
SHCK
DIPSY? LA-LA.
I'M IN...

DISPY, PO.

HE'S OUT.

CONFIRMED.

IT BETTER *ALL* BE THERE.

NOW SHOVE *OFF*.

GLADLY.

THANK YOU FOR A *LOVELY* STAY.

RIGHT, LET'S HAVE IT.

ANY TROUBLE?

NICK HERE COULD HAVE RUN THROUGH THE LOBBY *NAKED*, THEY WOULDN'T HAVE *NOTICED*.

I TOOK SHOTS OF *EVERYTHING* I FOUND, ALL THE PAPER.

THERE WAS A *LAPTOP*, BUT I THOUGHT HE MIGHT *NOTICE* IF THAT WENT MISSING.

LET'S HOPE THE *PAPER* WAS *ENOUGH*.

WHAT'S THE *NATIONAL* LANGUAGE OF ZIMBABWE?

ENGLISH, ACTUALLY, THOUGH TWO-THIRDS OF THE COUNTRY SPEAK SHONA, A BANTU DIALECT.

WHY?

SOME OF THE *PAPERS* WERE IN ARABIC, THAT'S *ALL*.

WHAT?

PAUL, COME IN.

I WAS *HOPING* TO HEAR FROM YOU OVER THE *WEEKEND.*

I HAD TO WAIT UNTIL D-INT WAS BACK IN HIS OFFICE THIS MORNING.

THIS WAS TRANSLATED BY THE NORTH AFRICA DESK.

SOURCE?

DAVID MWAMA'S *PERSONAL* PAPERS, AS PHOTOGRAPHED IN HIS HOTEL ROOM.

INDEED?

SPARE MY *EYES* THE MISERY OF *SMALL PRINT,* PAUL, AND TELL ME WHAT IT SAYS.

IT'S A *DRAFT* EXPORT AGREEMENT, ORCHESTRATED BY MWAMA, TO BE EFFECTED AT THE TIME HE SUCCEEDS ROBERT MUGABE AS *PRESIDENT* OF ZIMBABWE.

EXPORTING *WHAT?*

OIL. TO LIBYA.

I SEE.